Number Fifteen
*Carolyn and Ernest Fay Series in Analytical Psychology*

David H. Rosen, General Editor

The Carolyn and Ernest Fay edited book series, based initially on the annual Fay Lecture Series in Analytical Psychology, was established to further the ideas of C. G. Jung among students, faculty, therapists, and other citizens and to enhance scholarly activities related to analytical psychology. The Book Series and Lecture Series address topics of importance to the individual and to society. Both series were generously endowed by Carolyn Grant Fay, the founding president of the C. G. Jung Educational Center in Houston, Texas. The series are in part a memorial to her late husband, Ernest Bel Fay. Carolyn Fay has planted a Jungian tree carrying both her name and that of her late husband, which will bear fruitful ideas and stimulate creative works from this time forward. Texas A&M University and all those who come in contact with the growing Fay Jungian tree are extremely grateful to Carolyn Grant Fay for what she has done. The holder of the McMillan Professorship in Analytical Psychology at Texas A&M functions as the general editor of the Fay Book Series.

*Synchronicity*

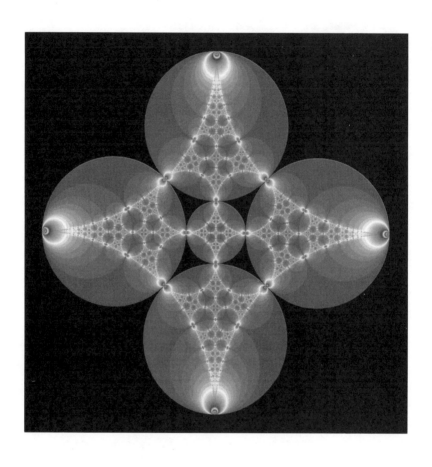

# Synchronicity

## Nature and Psyche
## in an Interconnected Universe

JOSEPH CAMBRAY

*Foreword by David H. Rosen*

Texas A&M University Press   College Station

This paper meets the requirements
of ANSI/NISO Z39.48-1992 (Permanence of Paper).
Binding materials have been chosen for durability.

LIBRARY OF CONGRESS CATALOGING-IN-PUBLICATION DATA

Cambray, Joseph.
Synchronicity : nature and psyche in an interconnected universe /
Joseph Cambray ; foreword by David H. Rosen. — 1st ed.
p. cm. — (Carolyn and Ernest Fay series in analytical
psychology ; no. 15)
Includes bibliographical references and index.
ISBN-13: 978-1-60344-143-8 (alk. paper)
ISBN-10: 1-60344-143-3 (alk. paper)
1. Coincidence.   2. Jung, C. G. (Carl Gustav), 1875–1961.   3. Field theory
(Physics)   4. System theory.   5. Complexity (Philosophy)
6. Empathy.   7. Democracy—Psychological aspects.   I. Title.   II. Series:
Carolyn and Ernest Fay series in analytical psychology ; no. 15.
BF175.5.C65C36   2009
150.19'54—dc22
2009011108

Cover image courtesy David Mumford, Caroline Senies, and David Wright, *Indra's
Pearls: The Vision of Felix Klein,* copyright © 2002, Cambridge University Press.
Figures 1, 6, and 7 courtesy Stiftung der Werke von C. G. Jung.
Figure 3 courtesy Jolande Jacobi, *The Psychology of C. G. Jung,* copyright © 1973,
Yale University Press.
Figure 4 courtesy Edward Edinger, *Anatomy of the Psyche,* copyright © 1985,
Open Court Publishing Company.

# Contents

# Illustrations

# Series Editor's Foreword

Everything is connected and the web is holy.

—Marcus Aurelius

In my back yard there is a Japanese garden with a pond containing numerous koi. Shortly before Joseph Cambray arrived to give his Fay Lectures in Analytical Psychology, which became this book, a snake caught and swallowed a koi. When I saw figure 1 of "Jung's carving of a snake swallowing a fish," I wondered if this was an example of synchronicity. By the lakeshore at Bollingen, Jung had found a snake that had choked in the act of swallowing a fish; both animals died. At the time Jung had been working on the symbolic relationship of the fish in Christianity and the snake in Alchemy. This incident struck a chord with me as the snake in my garden was at the edge of the pond but managed to swallow the fish, which was alive for several hours as its tail fin moved back and forth. I had not observed such an event before or after this occurrence.

In the introduction to this book Cambray defines synchronicity and links it to Jung's discovery of a science of the sacred, when nature and psyche come together. He describes synchronicity as a unique moment "falling together in time." Since I write haiku, I'm familiar with such moments when psyche and nature connect in a meaningful way. We actually characterize these as "haiku moments." For example, the haiku below was written when I was on a sabbatical at a Buddhist university in Japan. I was leaving the school to go home and stopped by a fishpond on the grounds; I saw that the koi made a moving circle, or mandala, which symbolizes wholeness.

*Ring of moving koi*
*In misty reflecting pool—*
*Full moon at sunset[1]*

Being in Japan, I felt like I had gone home. My being alone (a contraction of all One) was mirrored by the full moon and reflected in the pond by the ring of koi. I felt centered and at peace; this was a meaningful coincidence, or synchronicity.

This superb volume by Joseph Cambray helps us to connect nature and psyche and see that we live in an interconnected universe. The fact that his book comes at this time is an asymmetric synchronicity. It is an act of creation at the right moment. His work is scholarly and his background as a scientist and analyst enables him to incorporate many empirical findings that facilitate our understanding of the reality of synchronicity.

In chapter 1, "Synchronicity: The History of a Radical Idea," Cambray traces the origin of the concept of synchronicity to an early conversation between Jung and Albert Einstein and links it to the relativity of time and space. He helps us grasp the interaction of Jung and Wolfgang Pauli in their struggle to define and understand synchronicity. It was Pauli who helped Jung formulate the "psychoid archetype" that grounds the psyche in biology (and nature) and allows for interconnections with things in the universe. Add meaning to such a moment of interconnectedness and you have synchronicity. Jung's technique of active imagination facilitates the interconnection of psyche and nature and often results in a creative moment as well as an artistic product such as the haiku above. Cambray, being an analyst, allows us to see equanimity in a new light. It is a dance of subjectivity and objectivity in analysis. We mirror our patients and have subjective empathy, but we also break up the symmetry of the mirror and at times we experience "objective sympathy."[2] He documents how Jung's concept of synchronicity is linked to the *I Ching* of ancient Taoism, the origin of the universe, the psychoid archetype, psychic relativity, God, preestablished harmony in the monads of Gottfried Leibniz, the implicate order of David Bohm, and the Self (*imago Dei*) of Jung's psychology.

In chapter 2, "Interconnectedness: Visions and Science of Field Theory," Cambray explores how holism is critical to understanding synchronicity. In the holographic model the part leads to the whole. In Jung's view, we must integrate the shadow in order to move toward completeness, that is, individuation is a process toward wholeness. In Leibniz's monads, each one is like a mirror reflecting itself and others, as well as the whole universe. Cambray discusses Indra's Net from Indian and Chinese Buddhist philosophy as being similar in that each jewel reflects all jewels and the heavens. This parallels the individual ego glimpsing the Self (*imago Dei*) as the divine center and totality of the whole.

There is a return to holism in chapter 3 and a rebirth of a science of "Complexity, Emergence, and Symmetry." Cambray reveals how self-organization and emergence evolve out of complex adaptive systems. The role of symmetry and the need to break it to allow something new and asymmetric to emerge is discussed and illustrated clinically. He discusses Pauli's "mirror complex" and how Jung and Pauli saw parts of the whole in symmetric relationship with each other and how this helped them to break it and understand synchronicity.

The concepts of mirroring and resonance are explained in chapter 4, "Empathy and the Analytic Field," from a neuroscience level to a clinical one. Cambray brings up sympathy and relates it to a synchronistic dimension of empathy, which John Beebe, in his original and creative essay, describes as "objective sympathy."[3] Also in this chapter, Cambray discusses moral and ethical concerns about studying mirror neurons and imitative capacities.

In chapter 5, "Cultural Synchronicities," Cambray links previous concepts to the collective in an innovative manner. He discusses the emergence of democracy and Cortez's conquest of Mexico as collective and mythic examples of synchronicity. He also uses the discoveries of phosphorus and penicillin as historical and scientific instances of synchronicity and serendipity. Finally, in his "Afterword," Cambray circles back to his "Introduction" as a moment in time and to what is emerging on the individual, clinical, social, and global levels. He bridges nature and psyche and emphasizes how critical it is for all of us to be interconnected with the universe in personal and transpersonal ways.

It is noteworthy that Dr. Joseph Kerwin (the first physician astronaut in space and the science pilot of Skylab 2) was in attendance and even said a few words at the opening ceremony of Cambray's Fay Lecture Series on Synchronicity. Dr. Kerwin had his own moment of synchronicity while in space, "What struck me—during our space walk, when we spent the orbital 'night' just hanging on and watching the beautiful complexity of our world and the stars—was that I was seeing God's creation from a place few humans had seen it from. I was off the earth, in space: and it came home that this space filled the universe. I remembered reading C. S. Lewis's science fiction trilogy, in which 'Oyarsa' (close to our 'angel') ruled each planet but lived in space and had to dive into our atmosphere and hover there to talk to a human. When God became man he made a similar descent from here in space. That was a new thought, and a confirmation of my faith."[4]

In sum, this book is an accessible, thought provoking, and balanced scholarly treatise on synchronicity, and throughout this text it is possible to see synchronicity emerging in all its complexity.

*David H. Rosen*
*College Station, Texas*

# Acknowledgments

During the preparation of my Fay Lecture Series and this book on synchronicity it was my good fortune to have friends and colleagues from various analytic schools with whom I could openly discuss this emerging and complex topic. However, my first debt of gratitude is to my analysands, who in their persistence have taught me much; their processes have at times served as psychopomp to this book. As I traveled to places with various cultures I had the pleasure of presenting various papers on topics related to synchronicity and had valuable discussions with audiences in China, Italy, and Latin America, as well as across the United States and in the United Kingdom.

While I am not able to mention everyone who has been of assistance to me, I would like thank a few people who have added substantially to my reflections on the topic. Murray Stein offered insight on the ethical dimensions of synchronicity; Beverley Zabriskie was generous and helpful, especially regarding Pauli's contributions; Susan Gieser also provided valuable insights on Pauli. George Hogenson has been an invaluable discussant on the science behind these ideas, and David Tresan has enriched my understanding of the larger philosophical issues. John Beebe has graciously shared some of his remarkable knowledge of the *I Ching*. Hester Solomon has shared the passion for employing emergence to analytical psychology. Sam Naifeh has been especially helpful with the origins of democracy. Among those who have helped me in various ways I would like to mention Jean Knox, Tom Kirsch, Patricia Michan, Mario Saiz, Pilar Amezaga, and Caterina Vezzoli. I would like to thank Arlette Gillet for translating some of my work into Spanish. Similarly, Heyong Shen has provided opportunities to speak in China and has facilitated translation of several of my papers into Chinese. From the psychoanalytic community I would like to thank Peter Rudnytsky, the editor of *American Imago*, for his editorial input on my first article on synchronicity, which he published. Thomas Ogden has helped to explore the interconnections between psychoanalytic and Jungian ideas, especially on emergence. Lisby Mayer was a fellow traveler in this area and we had several memorable conversations about the potential value the synchronicity hypothesis could bring to psychoanalysis.

I wish to dedicate the book to my wife Linda, who has graciously lived through the writing process, reading the various drafts and providing wise counsel on many occasions. Her own clinical views have greatly enriched mine, and she often has provided counterpoint to ideas in formation. We have also shared many curious and meaningful coincidences.

My deep gratitude goes to David Rosen and Carolyn Fay for making this lecture and book series possible and for offering me the opportunity to present the lectures for 2008. It has been an honor and privilege to participate in this remarkable series. David has been the consummate host and a generous editor, with whom it has been a pleasure to work; his skills have truly enhanced the text. The students and faculty at Texas A&M were a delight to get to know, and the audience at the lectures engaged in ways that brought out the best in what I had to offer. I truly appreciate their insightful comments and questions. Finally, I wish to thank Texas A&M University Press for their leadership in the publishing community; their decision to provide online availability of this series demonstrates a twenty-first-century attitude that I hope other presses will follow.

*Synchronicity*

# Introduction

The impetus for this book arose out of clinical work. Analytic explorations have the potential to activate, energize, and focus unconscious processes, which often lead to experiences that are perceived as extraordinary from the perspective of ego consciousness. As I began to notice clusterings of such activations around certain themes and clinical situations, with some similarity to what Jung discussed in formulating his concept of synchronicity, I felt the need to reexamine his notion in light of new models of the mind and changes in scientific understanding. The challenge was to formulate my thoughts about it from both clinical and theoretical perspectives against the backdrop of Jung's profound reflections on the topic. Fortunately this coincided in time with the emergence of the field of complexity studies, allowing me to bring my background in the sciences into dialogue with my work as an analyst in a way that felt fresh and fruitful. Then the very act of working on this material in which I sought to describe and analyze these experiences seemed to become embedded in and a part of the experiences themselves, forcefully impressing me with the interconnectedness of our world.

Synchronicity as "a meaningful coincidence" and "an acausal connecting principle"[1] was a provocative hypothesis when it first was published and has remained so up to the present. In it C. G. Jung aimed at expanding the Western world's core conceptions of nature and the psyche. By requiring that we include and make room for unique individual experiences of life in our most fundamental philosophical and scientific views of the world, Jung challenged the status quo, urging us to go beyond the readily explainable, beyond the restrictions of a cause-effect reductive description of the world, to seeing the psyche as embedded into the substance of the world. As in so many of his ideas and projects, his genius resided in his capacity to see great depth in the odd, curious, and seemingly erroneous aspects of existence. This was already evident in his first research efforts, studying mediums; then examining the associations of the insane, discovering meaningful narrative fragments in what others discarded as only nonsensical. His was a mind open to exploring the possibility of meaning in chance or random events, deciphering if and when meaning might be present even if outside of conscious awareness.

In these endeavors Jung was radically transgressive; he cared little for the confines or boundaries of different disciplines but sought the most profound patterns in mind, culture, and nature, what he called "archetypes." Science and religion were not inherently opposed, and he discovered a science of the sacred, especially in his clinical work. Late in life, Jung wrestled with a formulation of synchronicity, and he drew upon the full breadth of his experience. He also chose Wolfgang Pauli as his coauthor for the 1952 book *The Interpretation of Nature and the Psyche*, in which he placed his major piece on synchronicity.[2] Pauli was a Nobel laureate in physics, and one of the founders of quantum theory as well as one of Jung's most dynamic correspondents.[3] It is the profound engagement with science, in part through his letters and dialogues with Pauli, that I will explore in the first chapter.

As a fuller grasp of the role of modern science in Jung's thinking is articulated, some of the relevant scientific, cultural background in which Jung was educated will also be explored in the first chapter. Holistic perspectives on natural phenomena were crucial to Jung's thought and to contextualizing his views on the new ideas in science emerging at the time. Relativity and quantum theories especially help place his thinking in a broader frame. The significance of field theories, in their classical and relativistic forms, for Jung's thought is discussed in chapter 2, along with amplifications that point to the archetypal background to these ideas.

Following this, there is a turn toward contemporary developments of related ideas, many of them occurring beyond Jung's lifetime. It can be argued that Jung's theories, practices, and clinical methods bear direct relationship to what currently is referred to as *complexity theory*. In particular, complex adaptive systems with their capacity for self-organization and emergence will be discussed in the third chapter.

The special role of symmetry and the importance of reducing or breaking symmetry for emergence to occur will be presented here at some length for the first time in terms of Jungian theory. A view of the universe as thoroughly interconnected arises out of this approach, and an attempt will be made to link this directly with personal experience.

In the fourth chapter these ideas will be brought to bear on the concept of empathy, which is experiencing a renaissance in psychology. Resonant phenomena between Self and Other have long been recognized in the analytic encounter and now are finding neuroscientific support. As empathic understanding is re-visioned, a Jungian field model will offer archetypal and synchronistic dimensions, permitting a range of insights not otherwise available.

Moving from dyadic to more collective phenomena, the application of the concepts developed in the previous chapters will be employed in chapter 5 to reconsider various historical events for their synchronistic aspects. In particular, "cultural synchronicities" are postulated for meaningful coincidences that effect large numbers of people either within a culture or at the meeting of cultures. For example, the origins of democracy in ancient Athens will be examined to find a model of group decision-making based on emergentist principles with a synchronistic core. This has applicability to contemporary organizational life. A variety of other encounters either between cultures, such as occurred during the conquest of Mexico, or at the edge of paradigm shifts, as with the rise of modern science in the seventeenth century, will be used to explore the utility of the concept of synchronicity applied to events that often unfold only over time and across various lives.

The personal dimension of this work has been deeply meaningful as well as fascinating to watch as it has unfolded. Originally educated as a scientist working at the edge of chemistry and physics, it has not always been an easy task for me to bridge that training with my psychotherapeutic practice as a Jungian analyst. The ideas developed at places such as the Santa Fe Institute, a "think tank" on complexity theory, opened up new ways that allowed me to retain a sense of integrity toward both professions and to envision a means of linking them. Thus the interconnections I sought span from the personal to the cosmological.

Pursuing these links resulted in a variety of peculiar experiences that offered direct insight into what Jung was presenting in his synchronicity essay. My attention to the topic was focused initially by clinical work with trauma survivors, some of whom exhibited a remarkable number of synchronistic occurrences during the course of analysis, which I have reported on in other publications.[4] As I began to grapple with the communicative value of these experiences and to see ways in which contemporary scientific writings on emergence might be pointing to a common ground, I had a number of experiences of synchronicities related to the writing of the material. Thus, I give one example embedded within a series of events: as I was in the midst of formulating these ideas for the first time, I was traveling back from Europe on a nearly empty plane (this was shortly after 9/11) where I was seated next to an individual who, unbeknownst to me, had a personal link to a statistician whose work questioning synchronicity I was in the middle of evaluating. This was meaningful in several ways; first we were probably the only two strangers sitting adjacent to each other, as the plane was quite empty and people were widely spaced except for couples. Then there was the content of the discussion that evolved. I had been working on unrelated material having to do with some organizational meetings I had attended, not on the synchronicity paper, so that when the person next to me began to chat I was initially resistant to engaging, but his exuberance won me over and I listened to and engaged in a discussion about some ideas he was interested in. Only gradually did I come to realize he might be knowledgeable about the statistics topic I was concerned with. Reluctant to raise details I made a couple of passing remarks and soon found I had the rather unexpected but welcome opportunity to discuss an area that was troubling me with someone who might be able to dialogue with me about it. And so we proceeded to discuss the problem, including the significance of our meeting as an instance of the subject under study. There were other features to the encounter that heightened the sense of interconnectedness, but confidentiality precludes my saying more. While I have flown many times since then, as well as continuing to work on the topic, never has another conversation on these matters emerged.

While these chapters are not meant to be the final or even the definitive word on synchronicity, I trust that you will find them thought provoking. I believe the best of analytic ideas need to be reexamined at least every generation to stay relevant, so that they remain living ideas. This text reflects my struggle to do so, at least for myself and I hope for some readers.

## CHAPTER 1

# Synchronicity:
# The History of a Radical Idea

The experience of synchronicity as coincidence(s) without causation, as commonly understood, yet having meaning to those involved, is well known to clinicians and those who explore unconscious processes. Anecdotal evidence concerning anomalous experience in therapeutic work in dynamic psychotherapy has gained interest and even some acceptance in recent years. For example, psychoanalyst Elizabeth Lloyd Mayer in a recent book describes how she and psychologist Carol Gilligan ran a surprisingly popular series of discussion groups at the biannual meetings of the American Psychoanalytic Association. These groups were oversubscribed despite their having made "attendance contingent on submitting a written account of an apparently anomalous experience, personal or clinical;"[1] the groups "teemed with impeccably credentialed professionals eager to tell stories . . . they normally didn't feel safe enough to divulge;"[2] many of the anecdotes recorded are from quite well known clinicians and analysts. However, Mayer only makes passing reference to Jung, and no reference to synchronicity is made. This is an avoidance based on politics rather than knowledge, as she had previously published reflections on synchronicity in the *Journal of Analytical Psychology* (*JAP*),[3] as well as delivering a lecture that included some discussion of synchronicity at the 2003 *JAP* conference "Science and the Symbolic World," held in Charleston, South Carolina. As we will see, Jung was obviously many years ahead of his time in terms of what clinicians were willing to reveal about such experiences. His courage in pioneering these studies deserves broader recognition and serious study.

Jung did provide some paradigmatic clinical experiences about synchronicity. His most famous example was of a young woman whose analysis was in a bit of impasse based on her resistance to the notion of unconscious process until she had a dream that included a golden scarab (as a piece of jewelry). In discussing the dream, Jung was alerted to a tapping sound at his window, which he opened. He caught a rose chafer, a Scarabaeid beetle, that he gave to the woman, apparently breaking through her resistance.[4] However, Jung was not content to collect anecdotes, he was a consummate theoretician who saw in these curious phenomena a window into understanding nature and the psyche in a new way. In this first chapter we will explore his thought on this idea.

Beginning with the term itself, *synchronicity,* how did Jung define and understand this most complicated idea? What material in his background did the notion connect with; what aspects of his training and experience were significant? How did it evolve over time in Jung's thinking, and what were some of the influences on this? A goal is to better understand why Jung felt the need to write his essays on this subject. As we progress through the material we will also look at what a contemporary view might be and of what relevance the concept might be.

Starting with the historical records in Jung's writings and lectures as we now have them, the first reference to the idea of synchronicity occurs on 28 November 1928 in Jung's seminars on dreams published in *Dream Analysis.*[5] Here he is discussing coincidences associated with dream imagery, specifically of a bull and bullfighting—in a previous class this had been a topic of discussion in exploring amplifications based on a patient's dream, which, however, was on a different subject. During that class there was a presentation by one of the seminar participants (Dr. Shaw) of a relevant dream from the night *before* the initial discussion but directly on the amplificatory topic. Meanwhile, the patient had during this time inexplicably produced drawings of a bull's head with the solar disc between the horns. In addition Jung had received a letter in the mail from a friend in Mexico who had just been to a bullfight—the letter was posted about the time of the class when the topic was first broached. In response to the clustering of these events Jung speaks of the dream as a "living thing" but notes it would be "a mistake to consider them as causal; events don't come about *because* of dreams, that would be absurd, we can never demonstrate that; they just happen" with "a sort of irrational regularity."[6]

This same year, 1928, Jung's interest in the Orient intensified—he had received *The Secret of the Golden Flower* from his friend and colleague, the sinologist and translator of the *I Ching*, Richard Wilhelm, this year. In the seminar under discussion he makes explicit reference to the East (meaning Chinese thought, especially Taoism):

> The East bases much of its science on this irregularity and considers coincidences as the reliable basis of the world rather than causality. *Synchronism* is the prejudice of the East; causality is the modern prejudice of the West. The more we busy ourselves with dreams, the more we shall see such coincidences—chances. Remember that the oldest Chinese scientific book [the *I Ching*] is about the possible chances of life.[7]

By December of 1929 Jung is explicitly using the term *synchronicity* in the seminar. Referring to another clustering of images from non-participants that mirrors class contents he notes: "They took up the symbolism as if they had been here with us. Since I have seen many other examples of the same kind in which people not concerned were affected, I have invented the word synchronicity as a term to cover these phenomena, that is, things happening at the *same moment* as an expression of the *same time content*."[8]

The following year Jung made his first public proclamation of the term at the memorial address for Wilhelm: "The science of the *I Ching* is based not on the causality principle but on one which—hitherto unnamed because not familiar to us—I have tentatively called the synchronistic principle."[9] Thus we see that Jung's initial formulations of the term drew upon his teaching and clinical experiences, especially with dreams and the way events associatively related to them cluster or form a network. He then seeks to understand systemically these immediate personal encounters in terms of scientific and philosophical principles. The inability of Western science as he sees it at this time to address such phenomena spurs him to look to sources from the East and, as we shall see, from the prescientific Western world.

While Jung continued to use and develop the term in his published works and in his letters, he did not produce a full-scale work on the topic until his 1951 Eranos lecture "On Synchronicity," which was itself drawn from the more complete essay "Synchronicity: An Acausal Connecting Principle," which he first published in 1952 in German as the first half of a book translated into English in 1955, *The Interpretation of Nature and the Psyche;* it was also published as a monograph in 1960 and is included in his Collected Works. The second half of the book contained an essay by Pauli, "The Influence of Archetypal Ideas on the Scientific Theories of Kepler."[10] As we have come to learn from historians in the field, Pauli and Jung had a significant correspondence from 1932 until Pauli's death in 1958.[11]

Pauli, who was a professor at the ETH (Eidgenössische Technische Hochschule [Swiss Federal Institute of Technology]) in Zurich had initially been referred to Jung as a patient by his father for emotional problems and his alcohol use in the wake of the suicide of his mother and the breakup of his first, brief marriage. Jung referred him to a junior colleague (Dr. Erna Rosenbaum) while in effect serving as supervisor and observing the process once removed, thus softening the boundaries between him and Pauli. The analysis was brief, eight months total, with ten months' worth of dreams collected, from which were selected the group that served as the basis for Part II of *Psychology and Alchemy (Collected Works 12)*. The exact nature of the relationship between the two men for the next several years remains in question, but they gradually transitioned the relationship into a friendship and a working partnership. Pauli was somewhat unique among Jung's correspondents with his ability to engage and challenge Jung in ways that truly altered his thinking. Recent scholarship has provided us with a more detailed understanding of the Jung/Pauli relationship. In particular, the letters between the two men have been translated into English available in book form,[12] and an excellent historical study of the significance of their dialogue on the way the concept of synchronicity was articulated has been published by Suzanne Gieser.[13] Pauli's influence on Jung's view of synchronicity is most germane here.

Pauli was a major force in convincing Jung to write the monograph, including the enticement of copublishing it along with his own essay. He also read and critiqued Jung's manuscript draft of his monograph and in the process significantly altered Jung's views on a number of topics, including archetypes. In examining Jung's formulation of synchronicity some of Pauli's main influences will be identified. Other sources of influence on Jung's thinking will be explored after the basic concepts are in hand.

### The Monograph: Synchronicity—An Acausal Connecting Principle

In his foreword Jung begins by acknowledging the difficulties that have kept him from publishing this material to date. These include feelings of inadequacy, especially of his scientific training (obviously he was bolstered by publishing together with Pauli; however, he was never comfortable with math and physics, his background was in the biological sciences). He cites three reasons for proceeding: (1) His increasing experience of and with the phenomena. (2) His research into the history of fish symbolism (presented in detail in his book *Aion*), which included a set of synchronicities—in addition to those in the published accounts, Jung found a snake that had choked in the act of swallowing a fish so that both had died. This occurred in 1933 at the shore by his Bollingen retreat. According to a family member, Jung saw this as a synchronicity since he was working on the relationship of Christianity/Fish and Alchemy/Snake at the time, and the external event paralleled his views on how these systems' inability to integrate their perspectives was fatal to each, leaving them dead. This conjunction so impressed Jung that he carved the image of the snake swallowing the fish into a block of stone that serves as part of the base for the loggia at Bollingen (fig. 1). (3) His realization that he had been "alluding to the existence of this phenomenon on and off in my writing for twenty years without discussing it any further."[14]

The first chapter, "The Exposition," immediately moves into modern physics, with an awareness that "[n]atural laws are statistical truths," that is, they are true at the macroscopic level, but do not hold

*Figure 1. Jung's carving of a snake swallowing a fish. Permission from Paul & Peter Fritz AG Literary Agency for the C. G. Jung Estate. Courtesy Stiftung der Werke von C. G. Jung*

for individual events at very small dimensions and time frames or very high velocities, that is, where relativistic and quantum phenomena are observed and prediction becomes increasingly uncertain; thus reality can only be described probabilistically. Since the Western scientific tradition up until the early twentieth century had been based on the view that natural laws were governed by causality, Jung now can claim that this is "only statistically valid and only relatively true."[15]

Jung's concerns are with events at a human scale that are rare or unique, and so nonreproducible, which he feels puts them outside the purview of the science of his day. He steps away from biology (his most familiar scientific realm) "where causal explanations often seem very unsatisfactory—indeed well-nigh impossible,"[16] despite his having employed biological examples to help with his understanding of instinctual and archetypal forces. Later we will reexamine this choice from a contemporary perspective.

Warming to his task, Jung next turns to the subject of chance, especially where causal connections between chance events seem preposterous. He acknowledges Paul Kammerer's work on "the law of series" but ultimately finds it uninteresting as it "contains nothing but runs of chance whose only 'law' is probability"[17] and are essentially meaningless.[18] However, now Jung can begin to assert his own ideas. He presents a cluster of six events that he observed around the figure of the fish, several of them wholly unrelated to the others, and notes the meaningful coincidence with an acausal connection. He also reports his subjective experience, identifying it as having a numinous quality. Thus he has given three key elements in his understanding of synchronicity: meaningful coincidence, acausal connection, and numinosity.

Contextualizing his views, Jung refers to Schopenhauer's "On the Apparent Design in the Fate of the Individual."[19] Claiming this as "standing godfather to the views I am now developing," here we can recognize Pauli's influence. While Jung had read Schopenhauer as an adolescent, Pauli brought this reference to Jung's attention and suggested its inclusion when he was critiquing the draft of the essay. Pauli describes a metaphoric model Schopenhauer offers for the interface of chance and necessity: "He compares causal chains with the meridians, simultaneousness with parallel circles—corresponding exactly to your 'equivalent cross-connections.'" Schopenhauer had in turn borrowed from Leibniz, seeing the kinds of connections he was describing as having a "pre-established harmony."[20] This model would form a highly ordered, regular, organized global network, a useful starting place but ultimately a form that was probably too rigid to fully serve Jung's purposes, as can be inferred from the arguments of chapter 3 where application of scale-free networks seem more suited to Jung's vision.

When Jung subsequently turns to J. B. Rhine's work on parapsychology done at Duke University (Rhine was a correspondent of Jung's), he notes the impact of affect on the results and how lack of interest and boredom have a negative effect on results; Jung will import this observation into the synchronicity hypothesis. Pauli, however, was uncomfortable with Jung's use of Rhine's work, referring, in a telling manner, to how it

seem[s] to me to be a totally different type of phenomenon from the other phenomena listed by you as "synchronistic." For with the former I cannot see any archetypal basis (or am I wrong there?). This for me, however, is crucial to an understanding of the phenomena in question as is your earlier observation ... that their appearance is complementary to the archetypal contents becoming conscious. I regret very much that this aspect is not mentioned at all in your latest work. Perhaps you could make further additions here.[21]

The archetypal hypothesis is reinserted into Jung's writing at this point, as the formal factor in organizing unconscious processes and providing the affective charge that can manifest in the feeling of numinosity referred to previously. However, Jung does not include the criticism about Rhine, ironically what Pauli says here bears some resemblance to Jung's dismissal of Kammerer's work, but Jung sees other possibilities in Rhine's results. In addition, Jung's fascination with parapsychological phenomena goes back to his childhood, with various uncanny events, especially surrounding his mother and then again when studying spiritism in a medium (his cousin) for his medical dissertation—see Charet[22] and Main[23] for some discussions of this source of early influence on Jung's formulation of synchronicity. In *Memories, Dreams, Reflections* Jung reports a number of incidents throughout his life, from childhood through old age, that could be viewed as parapsychological or synchronistic; these can and should be differentiated, however, as parapsychological events presume a causal explanation, based on unknown forces or "paranormal causality,"[24] while synchronicity would remain strictly acausal.

I will not go through the various criticisms of Rhine's work that have arisen over the years but instead note that Jung uses this material in conjunction with his synchronicity hypothesis to dismiss causality on the grounds that these kinds of phenomena cannot be understood in terms of *energy* but as "a falling together in time, a kind of simultaneity,"[25] which then becomes the reason for his choice of the term *synchronicity*. In another publication[26] I have examined this hypothesis regarding energy and have shown that the constraints Jung was applying (from nineteenth-century views of thermodynamics of systems at equilibrium) should be reconsidered in the light of the study of open systems, far from equilibrium, such as all forms of life, that can dissipate energy to create order locally. This in turn leads to the study of self-organizing systems within complexity theory as will be explored in chapter 3. Comprehending synchronistic events beyond the notion of chance or manifestations of probability associated with large numbers, as is typically done by mathematicians,[27] was something Pauli was able to address directly with Jung.[28]

The formulation of synchronicity in terms of simultaneity is, however, also riddled with difficulties. Several authors have noted that Jung's own examples often violate this definition, as with "precognitive" or predictive dreams—where an event is dreamed about often long before the outer occurrence. However, he attempts to retain the idea through various different strategies, including the problematic notion that "synchronistic events rest on the *simultaneous occurrence of two different psychic states*"[29]—for a critique of this see Roderick Main.[30] Pauli again raised concerns in his reading of the manuscript version; he was dismayed by the supposition of simultaneity: "The word 'synchron' thus seems to me somewhat illogical, unless you wish to relate it to a chronos that is essentially different from normal time."[31] Jung seems to be straining to use Einsteinian relativity theory but without sufficient grasp of the math and physics involved; as we will see in chapter 2, Pauli is uncomfortable with Jung's understanding of relativistic field theory.

Perhaps even more interesting for us at this point is Pauli's linking Jung's use of time with his concept of the "psychoid": "inasmuch as 'synchronistic' events form what you have termed a 'psychoid' initial stage of consciousness, it is understandable if (not always, but in many cases) they also share this standard characteristic of simultaneity. This also suggests that the meaning-connection, as primary agent, produces time as the secondary one."[32]

The notion of the psychoid was coined around 1907–8 by the biologist and neovitalist Hans Driesch in his Gifford lectures; he used it as "the basis of instinctive phenomena" in a vitalistic sense;[33] from him it is a nonphysical entity, a potential in the psyche with intensive, qualitative properties but without extension. Although Jung's borrowing of the term traces to Driesch, he employed it in a significantly different manner, as well as differentiating his use from how his former chief at the Burgholzli, Eugen Bleuler, used it as a kind of "cortical soul," and Jung himself did not employ it until 1946.[34] There he intends it as "quasi-psychic" at the interface where the psychological and material are undifferentiated and incapable of reaching consciousness as such; it operates prior to any Cartesian-like separation of mind and body, rather like an aspect of the *unus mundus* of alchemy, the unitary world at the fundament of our world. Curiously, some cosmologies of the premodern era, such as the alchemical one, parallel that of subatomic physics with an original state prior to any differentiation of substances. They present a world of relations rather than objects, that is, attending to the interconnectedness of all things, where interactive processes appear more fundamental than discrete particles.

In the above passage, Pauli's reframing of "simultaneity" in synchronicity in terms of "meaning-connection" with the time link as derivative opens a relativistic perspective. This, I believe, potentially subverts the independence of either connection in itself but instead leaves us with a psychologically relevant "meaning-time," which might more aptly be described as a *moment of complexity* compared with Jung's "falling together in time" or the quality of a "moment of time"; time would become an aspect of the moment of complexity, reminiscent of the way it is a component of relativistic space-time.

Pauli's suggestion does help Jung reconsider the notion of qualitative time as found in the *I Ching*, or more generally in prescientific cultures. Grappling with the new worldview arising through physics in the first half of the twentieth century Jung remarks:

But if space and time are only apparently properties of bodies in motion and are created by the intellectual needs of the observer, then their relativization by psychic conditions is no longer a matter for astonishment but is brought within the bounds of possibility.[35]

And a bit later:

when an event is observed without experimental restrictions, the observer can easily be influenced by an emotional state which alters space and time by "contraction"[36]

The influence that Einstein had on Jung in addition to Pauli is evident here, as well as Jung's tendency to borrow from physics without truly understanding it, as will be discussed in the next chapter. In correspondence with Carl Seelig after the publication of the synchronicity monograph, Jung explicitly identified Einstein as a houseguest on several occasions;[37] we know that one of these meetings was in early January 1911. This was in the period between Einstein's articulation of the Special and the General theories of relativity. A time when Einstein was engrossed in working through the details of his relativistic field theory, including the effects of gravitation. To Seelig, Jung comments:

It was Einstein who first started me off thinking about a possible relativity of time as well as space, and their psychic conditionality. More than thirty years later this stimulus led to my relation with the physicist Professor W. Pauli and to my thesis of *psychic synchronicity*.[38]

This psychic relativism is then linked to the underlying affect associated with the archetypal energies engaged: "Meaningful coincidences . . . seem to rest upon an archetypal foundation. . . . Affectivity, however, rests to a large extent on the instincts, whose formal aspect is the archetype."[39] *Jung is seeking to create a theory of the world based on the psychoid archetype as an originary point from which the subjective and objective realms emanate.*

At play in this interface between modern physics and the psyche, as Jung has come to know it through his observations, is a longing for insight into creation. Synchronicity as an "act of creation in time" is another of his ways of aphoristically defining the term. The search for the origins of creation, of course, is one of the places of great tension in our society, as between religious and scientific perspectives.

A variety of theories of the origins and nature of the universe were developed in the wake of Einstein's papers on relativity. Because the general theory of relativity leads to either an expanding or contracting universe, which Einstein considered wrong, he introduced the "cosmological constant" (in effect a "fudge factor") to preserve a static universe. Later he was to regret this, calling it the "biggest blunder" of his life. I will give a few details of the controversies in cosmology from 1922 through the 1950s (for a detailed study see *Big Bang* by Simon Singh, 2004), which would include the time frame for Jung's formulations of the synchronicity hypothesis.

In 1922 a Russian mathematician, Alexander Friedmann, published an article in which he looked at a variety of values for the cosmological constant including zero. The results without the constant lead to a dynamic, evolving cosmos, which Friedmann explained as "having been kick-started with an initial expansion, so it would have an impetus with which to fight against the pull of gravity;"[40] his view was of origin from a single point. Einstein retaliated with a letter of complaint but was forced to retract this when Friedmann's results proved to be sound mathematically. Because the journal was not well known, Einstein's apology was not widely disseminated, and when Friedman died several years later his name had slipped below the horizon of scientific notables. However, affect was building around what vision of the universe would prevail; complexes were activated in the scientific community.

The view of a dynamic, expanding universe was next put forward independently by Georges Lemaître, a Belgian who was both a physicist and a priest. Lemaître realized that the equations of general relativity lead to a moment of creation and proposed an extremely compact starting point he called the "primeval atom."[41] In sketching out details as he understood them, Lemaître gave the first scientific description of what would become the Big Bang model in 1927 at the Solvay conference. According to Singh, Einstein informed him of Friedmann's work while again rejecting the model: "Your calculations are correct, but your physics is abominable."[42] Discouraged, Lemaître abandoned any attempt to promote his theory. However, several years later Edwin Hubble reported the observation of the galactic red-shift, demonstrating that galaxies were in recession from one another. With help from Arthur Eddington, Lemaître's views were now acclaimed, and on a visit to Hubble's labs at the Mount Wilson observatory, where he could see the original data, Einstein issued a public statement in which "he renounced his own static cosmology and endorsed the Big Bang expanding universe model."[43] Einstein and Lemaître even appeared together at a seminar in Pasadena in 1933 to discuss Hubble's observation; Einstein now embraced Lemaître's work: "This is the most beautiful and satisfactory explanation of creation to which I have ever listened."[44] Nevertheless, controversy continued to rage.

By 1948 the cosmologist George Gamow, who had been a student of Friedmann's, offered what has come to be the predominate view, the "big bang" theory. Gamow elaborated and developed Lemaître's views based on his own interest in nucleosynthesis (forging of atoms beyond hydrogen in thermonuclear reactions). According to Singh:

> [Gamow] assumed that the initial components of the universe would have been separate protons, neutrons and electrons, the most fundamental particles known to physicists at the time. He called this "mix ylem" . . . a word he stumbled upon in Webster's Dictionary. This obsolete Middle English word means "the primordial substance from which the elements were formed." . . . In addition to the particles of matter, the early universe contained a turbulent sea of light.[45]

A striking resemblance to the *prima materia* of the chaos of creation of the alchemists, of which Jung was so fond, can be seen here. It should be noted that further refinements of the theory, which postulate an initial singularity, an indescribable state of infinite density and temperature where the known laws of physics are no longer valid and yet from which everything emerges, were not in the scientific discourse of this period, but come later.

In an ironic twist the name "Big Bang" was first suggested by Fred Hoyle during a set of five lectures he gave in 1950 on BBC radio—the transcripts were published in the *Listener* and later in Hoyle's book *The Nature of the Universe*. Hoyle was championing his "Steady State" model of the universe and was attempting to deride the dynamic, evolving model by dismissing it as the "Big Bang." Hoyle has particular importance for this chapter as we know Jung read *The Nature of the Universe*. He refers to it along with several other of Hoyle's books in his monograph on flying saucers.[46] Barbara Hannah also mentions Jung's having read two of Hoyle's books on cosmology.[47] While Jung was complimentary in a general way about Hoyle's work, his primary interest was in a science fiction novel of Hoyle's, *The Black Cloud*,[48] in which Jung saw culturally relevant mythic and alchemical ideas at play.[49] In a letter of January 1958 he told a correspondent that "the book is highly worthwhile, as it describes how the collective unconscious is coming to an astronomer. Very exciting!"[50] Jung's interest here was as a psychological observer, noting the way archetypal patterns enter culture and by implication science. Pauli had already warned him, through Aniela Jaffe who had sent Pauli a review of Hoyle's *The Nature of the Universe*, of the dangers of Hoyle's views on the steady state universe: "this type of cosmogony is *not physics but a projection of the unconscious.*"[51]

Although details of Jung's opinions on the controversy of scientific views on cosmogony are not directly available in the published letters and texts, it is clear that he was informed of the multiplicity of theories. He even differentiates himself from Einstein's views, as in a 1953 letter to James Kirsch:

> If God's consciousness is clearer than man's, then the Creation has no meaning and man no *raison d'être*. In that case God does not in fact play dice, as Einstein says, but has invented a machine, which is far worse. Actually the story of the Creation is more like an experiment with dice than anything purposive. These insights may well involve a tremendous change in the God-image.
>
> "Synchronicity" is soon to appear in English . . .[52]

I would suggest this juxtaposing of the "Synchronicity" essay is directly linked to Jung's evolving thoughts about Creation; not simply acts of creation in time but of cosmogony. He is also attempting to embrace quantum theory and relativity together in this passage; he is seeking an originary state. As previously noted, the scientific views of a singularity and the extremely early states of the universe, well before Gamow's *ylem*, would not have been available to Jung as science. However, from his knowledge of cultural history and using his profound intuition he seems to be moving toward a view in which space and time have not yet come into existence, in the time before matter and energy were separate—features of the first $10^{-36}$ seconds of the existence of the universe. Echoes of such ideas can be found in his remarks, such as:

> since experience has shown that under certain conditions space and time can be reduced to almost zero, causality disappears along with them because causality is bound up with the existence of space and time and physical changes, and consists essentially in the succession of cause and effect. For this reason synchronistic phenomena cannot in principle be associated with any conceptions of causality.[53]

Jung is speaking here about acausal coincident phenomena that are meaningfully linked, but the collapse of space and time together with the disappearance of the principle of causality is remarkably congruent with the best theories in physics for the origins of the universe. The point in this is to try and articulate what Jung may be reaching for with his theory of synchronicity. It is as if at the deepest level he is finding a place for the psyche at the origins of the universe through the psychoid archetype. This is not an intelligent design argument but an indication that the universe is as permeated with psyche as it is with space, time, and matter; that synchronicities provide traces of an original undifferentiated state. In such a cosmogony I suggest Jung is leading us to see psyche as another of the potentials inherent in the singularity. As the universe expands from the primordial singularity and cools, matter is separate from energy yet can interact with it (for example, as radiation) and space-time emerges; patterns begin to take shape and become substantial, first in the form of particles, which make up matter, then with greater cooling and expansion into clouds, which become stellar and galactic nurseries from which eventually the patterns that lead to life emerge and so on to consciousness, that is, patterns with the potential to form psyche and hold meaning. That Jung recognized such potentials within the context of evolution on earth is evident from his March 1959 letter to Erich Neumann:

> In this chaos of chance, synchronistic phenomena were probably at work, operating both with and against the known laws of nature to produce, in archetypal moments, syntheses which appear to us miraculous. . . . This presupposes not only an all-pervading, latent meaning which can be recognized by consciousness, but during that preconscious time, a psychoid process with which a physical event meaningfully coincides. Here the meaning cannot be recognized because there is as yet no consciousness.[54]

In this sense Jung's view is close to the work of David Bohm on the implicate order, though Bohm's view retrieves causality as hidden in this.[55] Psyche in this model serves as an ordering, organizing principle that we will explore at more length in the next chapter. The spiritual dimension of such an argument is not lost on Jung. By the end of the monograph he also re-envisions simultaneity through a theological metaphor: "what happens successively in time is simultaneous in the mind of God."[56] Points of origin seem to elicit the need to hold the tension between opposing views, which in turn allow emergent processes. The spiritual significance of synchronistic experiences has been aptly explored by Roderick Main in his recent works,[57] which include careful, detailed study of the critiques of science and religion contained within Jung's theory of synchronicity.

## Jung's Identified Forerunners to the Idea of Synchronicity

In the latter portion of "The Exposition" and then again in more detail in chapter 3 of his monograph Jung provides some of the historical background to his notion of synchronicity. We will first look at these explicitly identified sources and later will include some additional sources. Roderick Main[58] has helpfully identified eight areas of influence that contributed to Jung's thinking about synchronicity, some of which are explicitly used in the monograph, others are not. As the focus of this study is not the same as Main's, the influences I will point to are also different, and even when the same or similar sources are used, what is emphasized is distinct.

Citing a long passage from Albertus Magnus on magic, itself borrowing from a treatise of the tenth- to eleventh-century Persian physician/polymath Avicenna, which recognizes the role of emotion as the "cause" of such [magic] events, Jung seeks to provide a venerable philosophical pedigree for his new conception. This continues with a quote from Goethe, "We all have certain electric and magnetic powers within us and ourselves exercise an attractive and repelling force, according as we come into touch with something like or unlike."[59] Although Jung notes that this remains a precursor, as a form of magical thinking, he does not comment on the metaphors used—in the next chapter we will touch upon the late eighteenth- and early nineteenth-century's use of such conceptions from physics to explain psychological states. For the present it should be noted that Goethe's comments are from the last decade of his life (d. 1832), that is, they precede the scientific formulations of electrical and magnetic phenomena in terms of field theory as first articulated by Michael Faraday in 1845, which we shall see is directly relevant to Jung's ideas—a precursor that Jung does not explicitly identify but that is highly germane.

Jung goes on to make passing reference to the work of those later nineteenth-century scientists involved in the Society for Psychical Research (SPR), but his main attention is reserved for the *I Ching*, or *Book of Changes*, the ancient Chinese philosophical text with its divinatory method—he had of course also written the foreword to Wilhelm's translation of the *I Ching*, where he had presented some of his ideas on synchronicity.[60] From his reading Jung was struck by the capacity for an intuitive grasp of the whole of a situation that seemed to be offered in this oracle. For him the Chinese sages accordingly drew upon "the hypothesis of the unity of nature, [and] sought to explain the simultaneous occurrence of a psychic state with a physical process *as an equivalence of meaning*."[61]

Although he seeks to make an experiment with an intuitive-mantic technique and decides on astrology, Jung is not wholly comfortable with this, and the experiment itself relies on a statistical study of the marriage connection between individuals (a type of synastry). Pauli was politely discouraging about this entire project. Even though the results hold some interest in terms of the way the affective involvement of the researchers was implicated, these have tended to be muddled or misunderstood by various readers who would make Jung into a New Age guru.

After presenting the astrology experiment, Jung returns to the forerunners now with more detailed exploration of the philosophical side of Taoism. Wilhelm's translation of the Tao as "meaning" is key for Jung.[62] Lao Tzu's description of the nature of the Tao as "no-thing" (for example, We turn clay to make a vessel / But it is on the space where there is nothing that the utility of the vessel depends) is tied to meaning or purpose for Jung. He notes that "it is only called Nothing because it does not appear in the world of the senses, but is only its organizer;"[63] the capacity for organization, more exactly self-organization, as the source of synchronistic meaning is crucial and will be discussed at length in the next chapter.

Searching for a parallel in the history of Western thought, Jung moves to the medieval world with the theory of *correspondentia*, which, according to Cirlot, is

> founded upon the assumption that all cosmic phenomena are limited and serial and that they appear as scales or series on separate planes; but this condition is neither chaotic nor neutral, for the components of one series are linked with those of another in their essence and in their ultimate significance.[64]

We are reminded of Kammerer's series but with the addition of this essential and significant linkage between series. This theory is also often framed in terms of a microcosm/macrocosm link: As above, so below.

Curiously, in a footnote Jung also claims that Pauli had told him about Niels Bohr's use of the term *correspondence* "as a mediating term between the representation of the discontinuum (particle) and the continuum (wave),"[65] but here Jung has garbled Bohr's idea of complementarity, which does address the wave-particle duality of quantum systems, with Bohr's correspondence principle, which states that the behavior of quantum mechanical systems reproduce those of classical physics in the limit of large numbers of quantum systems. While I do not wish to belabor a minor semantic confusion on Jung's part, he had previously articulated a theory of dreams that relies more heavily on compensatory input to the conscious position than complementary information:

> Compensation must be strictly distinguished from *complementation.* The concept of a complement is too narrow and too restricting; it does not suffice to explain the function of dreams, because it designates a relationship in which two things supplement one another more or less mechanically. Compensation, on the other hand, as the term implies, means balancing and comparing different data or points of view so as to produce an adjustment or a rectification.[66]

And, in a footnote to this paragraph, he states: "This is not to deny the principle of complementarity. 'Compensation' is simply a psychological refinement of this concept." It might therefore be argued that correspondence, complementarity, and compensation are all working in the background of Jung's wrestling with his understanding of synchronicity together with quantum physics. His confusion may be due in part to the overwhelming complexity of the phenomena he is seeking to formulate—he wishes synchronicity to compensate causality and sees a complementary relationship between modern physics and psychology, trying to draw out the ways they correspond; his lack of formal training in physics and math again may have contributed to this confusion.

Behind the theory of correspondence, Jung locates the classical world's notion of the *sympathy of all things*. In this he turns to the Greek physician Hippocrates:

> There is one common flow, one common breathing, all things are in sympathy. The whole organism and each one of its parts are working in conjunction for the same purpose . . . the great principle extends to the extremist part, and from the extremist part it returns to the great principle, to the one nature, being and not-being.[67]

This is a model of a wholly or radically interconnected universe. Jung continues to amplify this viewpoint with a series of philosophers from the ancient world through to the Renaissance. The last and most useful for this study is Gottfried Wilhelm von Leibniz (1646–1716), who lived during and was very much a part of the transition from the medieval to the modern world.

Leibniz's notion of the "pre-established harmony," which was in part his rejoinder to Descartes' mind/body split, is particularly of interest to Jung. Leibniz was opposed to dualism, seeing mind and body as ultimately composed of the same substance, yet each remains metaphysically distinct without interaction. The idea is drawn from his theory of monads, the basic units of perceptual reality that form all substances; for Leibniz the soul was seen as a rational monad. To refute Descartes, Leibniz postulates monads as being wholly without interactions among themselves but having been initially coordinated by God in a preestablished harmony that keeps them in tandem with one another, linked but without causality. Leibniz used the simile of two synchronized clocks to explicate the mind/body coordination, an idea he likely borrowed from the Flemish philosopher Arnold Geulincx—Jung acknowledges that Pauli pointed out this borrowing to him, which in itself is not surprising given Pauli's vision of a highly complex world clock with two circles, a horizontal and a vertical one, each with several colors and a common center as well as three distinct pulses. Pauli identifies the vision as one of his own, along with the dream that had provoked it (in letter 23P; also see *Collected Works 12,* paragraphs 307ff. and *Collected Works 11*, paragraphs 112ff. for details of Jung's understanding of this imagery). Jung's reading of Leibniz focuses on how the monads are each an "active indivisible mirror," a microcosm with connections "which express all the others;" "a perpetual living mirror of the universe."[68]

Extending this, according to Leibniz: "Body and soul are so adapted that a resolution in the soul is accompanied by an appropriate movement in the body;" "the tendencies of the soul towards new *thoughts* correspond to the tendencies of the body towards new *shapes and motions*."[69] This psychosomatic parallelism caused Jung to acknowledge: "the possibility that the relation between body and soul may yet be understood as a synchronistic one. Should this conjecture ever be proved, my present view that synchronicity is a relatively rare phenomenon would have to be corrected,"[70] and he cites the work of C. A. Meier on this, which has been detailed in a previous publication[71] and will be discussed further in several of the following chapters.

Leibniz is also now credited with having been the person who first used the term *supervene* to refer to the mind-body relationship.[72] Although not used again in a similar fashion until the twentieth century, Leibniz's use of the term is consistent with the way it is employed in contemporary philosophy of mind, where it is the dominant view of the brain-mind relationship; it is roughly equivalent to the emergentist perspective in the neurosciences and in some philosophies.

Although Jung does not refer to it in his monograph, Leibniz is also known to have been the first major Western intellect to encounter the *I Ching*.[73] He was given a copy by a Jesuit missionary in China, Father Joachim Bouvet, in the course of a fascinating exchange of letters that included Bouvet's awareness of Leibniz's articulation of binary arithmetic and how this matched a version (the natural hexagram order) of the *I Ching* to which he had access. This version has the striking feature of being arranged in direct sequential order from 0 through 63 in base two if a broken line is taken for a zero and an unbroken line is taken as one. Leibniz's numbering of these hexagrams can be seen in reproductions of the diagrams sent to him by Bouvet.[74] The story of the Bouvet/Leibniz correspondence first came to light in 1943, published by none other than Richard Wilhelm's son, Helmut Wilhelm.[75]

He also presented this information at the last Eranos conference Jung attended in 1951, and we know Jung did hear the lecture because he makes a passing reference to it when he himself lectures.[76]

## Jung's Conclusion

The final section of the monograph is mostly devoted to discussing the need for the concept of synchronicity. Jung is especially concerned about psychophysical parallelism, including the mind/body problem and the expanded question of general acausal orderedness. The first issue he raises is "absolute knowledge," which he feels is "characteristic of synchronistic phenomena, a knowledge not mediated by sense organs," which in turn "supports the hypothesis of a self-subsistent meaning, or even expresses its existence."[77] This would be a form of unconscious knowing mediated by archetypal processes. As potential examples, Jung cites a variety of medical anecdotes of what we would call "out of body experiences" in which a seemingly comatose person later accurately describes events that occurred during the period they appeared unconscious. For Jung, "where sense perceptions are impossible from the start, it can hardly be a question of anything but synchronicity."[78] However, as a recent spate of neuroscientific research has demonstrated, this phenomenon is now becoming amenable to study and for the first time has even been induced in the laboratory at University College London, in healthy individuals, with recognition of possible beneficial applications like remote surgery through virtual techniques.[79] Whether the current neuroscience research will lead to new views of the mind/body interaction compatible with Jung's synchronicity hypothesis remains to be seen.

Jung's second example of noncerebral intelligence came from the then recently published study of *The Dancing Bees* by Karl von Frisch.[80] The purposeful, intelligent communicative power of the dance of bees providing navigational information to hive mates so as to locate a source of pollen was eye opening to Frisch and many others at the time. The adaptive intelligence of social insects was a subject of growing interest in the scientific community through the middle years of the twentieth century. As the field has developed, more explicit, detailed studies of what is now often called *swarm logic* have appeared in a variety of disciplines. These demonstrate "bottom up" organizational features with emergent properties, which will be discussed at greater length in the next chapter.

In the final portion of the conclusion Jung raises the question of the frequency of synchronicities, rare or common, and moves into a discussion of general acausal orderedness. For Jung this includes the properties of numbers (for example, consider prime numbers), radioactive decay, the possible relations between mind and body, and so on—the role of radioactivity in Jung and Pauli's correspondence and in the synchronicity hypothesis will be taken up when we look at symmetry. Jung's penchant for quaternities led him together with Pauli to suggest several diagrams for a re-visioning of Western science and philosophy (that is, Space and Time on the vertical axis with Causality and Synchronicity on the horizontal axis; Indestructible Energy and Space-Time Continuum on the vertical, and Constant Connection through Effect (Causality) and Inconstant Connection through Contingence, Equivalence, or "Meaning" (Synchronicity) on the horizontal (for precursors see Meier, *Atom and Archetype*, letters 45P and 46J). Recognizing that space and time form a single unit in relativity physics, Jung relies on the psychoid aspect of his archetypal theory to provide a bridge between causality and synchronicity:

> Archetypal equivalences [outer physical and inner psychic processes] are *contingent* to causal determination, that is to say there exist between them and the causal processes no relations that conform to law.... It is an initial state which is "not governed by mechanistic law" but is the precondition of law, the chance substrate on which law is based. If we consider synchronicity or the archetypes as the contingent, then the later takes on the specific aspect of a modality that has the functional significance of a world-constituting factor. The archetype represents *psychic probability* ...[81]

Thus synchronicity is leading Jung to an expansion of his archetypal theory, while at the same time he subsumes synchronicity as a special subset of general acausal orderedness. Previously Jung had differentiated the archetype-as-such (or "in-itself," a Kantian noumenon) from archetypal imagery, with the former assuming the more fundamental role so as to avoid any Lamarckian implications. The archetype-as-such is without form or content, only the potential to express, as in the axes of a crystal lattice, one of his metaphors for it. According to Gieser, Pauli also was helping to stress the shift in conception of the archetype away from being inborn or being an ideal form to something active, constellating rather than causing events. She reports Pauli's remarks that "the archetype should not be seen as an 'inborn structure' lying 'latent,' just waiting to manifest itself, but as something that constellates, or emerges at certain stages and situations in life."[82] Thus the concept is moving toward an emergentist view, and in the passage above it is the archetype-as-such that serves as the explanatory principle that would gain the status of a new paradigm. Within this view it becomes the deep background organizing force for all knowledge, of the physical and psychological universes; psychology itself becomes the guardian of the arts and sciences, holding the keys to cosmological as well as ontological secrets. Here we have a grand vision to which Jung is striving to give birth late in life. In several further chapters this accent on the emergent will be explored further.

## Value and Relevance of Synchronicity

The writing of the synchronicity essay seems to have served multiple purposes for Jung. With the rise of relativity and quantum theories, physics became the primary scientific discipline of the twentieth century, especially dominant in the first half of the century. Many of the world's best minds were fascinated by the new views of the world coming out of physics. In keeping with this, Jung wished to see psychology on similar footing and sought to engage the new concepts from the standpoint of his archetypal theory. He borrowed and transmuted the language of physics in an attempt to enlarge psychology while simultaneously seeking to use this same psychology to incorporate and extend physics itself. In the process his psychology was altered, archetypal theory was revised, the notion of the psychoid was given greater relevance, and a new pathway for exploring coincidences was opened. Jung's theories thus were changed by the encounters with Pauli and modern physics more generally in a manner reminiscent of Jung's own views of the therapeutic process in which both partners are altered:

> The relation between doctor and patient remains a personal one within the impersonal framework of professional treatment. By no device can the treatment be anything but the product of mutual influence. . . . For two personalities to meet is like mixing two different chemical substances: if there is any combination at all, both are transformed. . . . You can exert no influence if you are not susceptible to influence.[83]

As a theory, synchronicity therefore seeks to present a universal principle, something fundamental to the world, at the core of existence and not only human existence but of the world itself. Jung seeks to go beyond the descriptions of classical physics, as the best of his contemporaries in physics were doing, but using his psychological understanding to derive a compensatory notion to causality. This was guided in part by the project of articulating a holistic science, valuing the profound interconnectedness of all things. Discerning patterns of the whole that link disparate elements into a unity that cannot be adequately described by reductive approaches provided a perspective Jung felt was missing from the scientific worldview of his day. In the nineteenth century a similar vision had been sought by those following the *naturphilosophie* of the German Romantic tradition, but with few successes. With the aid of the revolution brought by modern physics, and in dialogue with some of its exponents, Jung brought the equally revolutionary psychology of the unconscious to bear on an emerging description of the world in which the psychological and the physical are inextricably intertwined.

Jung's search for an ordering principle at the origins of creation (natural and human) involves a great intuitive leap that has the potential to demonstrate the utility of a psychological approach to knowledge—previously I have discussed synchronicity as a theory of creativity at the edge of genius and madness.[84] In this, Jung's clinical experience together with his knowledge of unconscious patterns and dynamics alerted him to what was being avoided or ignored, left in the unconscious. He had a long history of recognizing and valuing those aspects or products of the mind that are too readily discarded or dismissed. His studies on the word association test had taught him the value of what was seen as errors, mistakes, slips of the tongue, and so forth, to be discarded by those who held a wholly rationalistic view of psychology. In contrast, reclaiming the meaning in these events, as well as in the speech of psychotic patients, had trained Jung to search for the significance of what others did not wish to see. Exploration of the clustering of bizarre coincidences or anomalous events around subjective meaning was an extension of this earlier work, though perhaps the most deeply challenging of Jung's attempts at theory building. By eschewing a statistical approach in studying human affairs, seeking to understand unique events, Jung was one of the first scientific psychologists to adopt what might now be called a qualitative phenomenological approach to research using clinical data.

As a creative act, developing the theory of synchronicity required Jung to go to the edges of his own knowledge as well as seeking the limits of his collaborators, especially Pauli. Just as the capacity for metaphor has been linked with the formation of mind, synchronicity could be treated as a specific kind of metaphor-forming process when reflected upon from outside the event—an "objective" metaphorizing tendency of the world itself. Disparate elements without apparent connection are brought together or juxtaposed in a manner that tends to shock or surprise the mind, rendering it open to new possibilities, for a broadening of the view of the world, offering a glimpse of the interconnected fabric of the universe.

## CHAPTER 2

# Interconnectedness: Visions and Science of Field Theory

Jung's monograph on synchronicity was the product of years of thinking; and he only published it in the last decade of his life. Various authors[1] have detailed how this idea fits into the corpus of Jung's other writings, how it is an integral part of analytical psychology (Jung's term for his general psychological approach). For present purposes, I would like to emphasize and develop a perspective that informs much of Jung's thinking: holism. I will try to build a context for locating Jung's idea of synchronicity based on the scientific milieu he was exposed to from late adolescence through his later years, in particular the influence of scientific holism. Jung himself only rarely refers directly to this milieu, and then mostly through specific figures that have captured his imagination, such as Goethe.

The term *holism* goes back to the ancient Greeks' Ολος/holos meaning whole, entire, complete; this was applied to one of the main horrors of the twentieth century, holo-caust: burnt whole. In his *Metaphysics* Aristotle states: "In the case of all things which have several parts and in which the totality is not, as it were, a mere heap, but the whole is something beside the parts, there is a cause;"[2] or in the shorthand of gestalt psychology: "the whole is greater than the sum of the parts." Throughout Western history there has been a tension, at times a complementarity, between holistic and reductionistic approaches to understanding the world. Reductionism is the method of breaking down something complex into its component parts and explaining its operations and functions through these components. Western science with its analytic paradigm has primarily focused on the explanatory power of the reductive approach, especially as this lends itself more readily to quantitative and mathematical treatments. Before exploring the countertradition of holism in science, the tendencies toward holism in Jung's writing will be discussed.

## Jung and Holism

While Jung does not use the term *holism* or its variants, he writes extensively about the value of "wholeness." Thus, his model of psychological health and maturation focuses on the integration of the personality. The process of individuation is a sustained dialectic that occurs through the conscious self, the sense of I, identifying, engaging and/or confronting unconscious dimensions of the personality. For example, unwanted or undesirable aspects of a person's psyche, which tend to be suppressed or repressed, often figure in dreams as shadow elements (these can be unsavory characters, menacing animals, and so forth). The work of analysis in the service of individuation will then require facing the distressing or upsetting contents, seeing how they belong to a person and when possible entering into a process of engaging the images as psychologically real, to be taken as seriously as an external encounter. Repeated engagements with the full range of images that arise from the unconscious can have a profound impact on both conscious and unconscious, as Jung details in his various writings, for example, in "A Study in the Process of Individuation;"[3] "Individual Dream Symbolism in Relation to Alchemy,"[4] as well as in numerous other places. Jung articulates typical stages in the individuation process, which can be found in various places but are codified in the second of his *Two Essays on Analytical Psychology.*[5]

In discussing individuation, becoming more fully oneself, Jung repeatedly points out that this is not a form of perfectionism but is about completeness; it requires finding ways to deal with all aspects of one's personality, positive and negative. Because Jung includes the undesirable aspects of personality, both individual and collective, the holistic goal tends to differ from that of morality, which is commonly found in many philosophical or religious systems that emphasize seeking only the good in oneself and the world.

Related to individuation is Jung's larger view of the Self, as the center and circumference of the entire personality, conscious and unconscious. For Jung the ego is merely the center of consciousness, while the Self is the archetypal potential from which the ego complex emerges. The Self serves as the deepest source of motivation for the unfolding and subsequent reunification of the personality; when expressed, its archetypal imagery coincides with the god image though it can also take the negative of this as in daimonic forms—from the ancient Greek, *daimon,* "a god, goddess, divine power, genius, guardian spirit."[6]

Jung notes Self imagery can range from inorganic forms (such as the alchemical *lapis* or crystalline structures) to animal, humanoid, and divine representations, all tending to appear with a numinous feeling tone (for a detailed look at the numinous from analytic perspectives see Casement and Tacey, eds., *The Idea of the Numinous*). Models of the development of the personality associated with this view have a trajectory beginning with ego emergence from the primal Self followed by the need for sustained interaction between ego and Self; psychopathology in this system is related to ruptures in the ego-Self axis.[7] For the present purposes, the Self appears as a paradoxical, quasi-religious entity for Jung, it is the central archetype but also encompasses the whole of the archetypal world, the collective unconscious, as well as the conscious personality; it clearly is a whole that cannot be described solely in terms of its parts and is not definable as a completely logistically consistent term.

The archetypes of the collective unconscious are of course an essential feature of Jung's model of the psyche. Virtual, empty forms in themselves, they're imagined as structuring all psychic life; when constellated, as through a matching of environmental and internal cues, they tend to manifest in archetypal imagery. They are psychosomatic entities linking body and mind. Taken together they form a highly interconnected polycentric network: "It is a well-nigh hopeless undertaking to tear a single archetype out of the living tissue of the psyche; but despite their interwovenness they do form units of meaning that can be apprehended intuitively."[8] Each archetype has numinous potential, and polytheistic cultures are seen to give expression to archetypal diversity (the Self as a single entity tends to be more directly associated with monotheistic cultures). Samuels and colleagues nicely capture a psychological reading of this: "Gods are metaphors of archetypal behaviors and myths are archetypal enactments."[9] We will return to the network aspect of Jung's model and to an emergentist reading a bit later.

Philosophically Jung was intrigued by binary oppositions, such as conscious/unconscious, day/night, and such, together with their compensatory relationships. The resolution of the psychological tension engendered from attempting to hold opposites in mind comes through the emergence of a third position, reminiscent of the Hegelian thesis, antithesis, synthesis. However, for Jung the third did not achieve wholeness until becoming a quaternity; fourfold structures were seen by him as balanced and complete, hence his celebration of the Catholic Church's decision in November 1950 to value the Assumption of Mary. For Jung this was a completing of the doctrine of the Trinity, with the addition of the feminine fourth—Jung's concern was not about theological dogma but about the psychological meaning of such statements.

As Jung developed his own unique methods for handling unconscious material, they too had a holistic focus to them. When first formulating his method of amplification in 1914 he explicitly stated that he was seeking a way to analyze that was not reductive but constructive.[10] By this point he is already differentiating his approach from a strictly causal one, referring to the human psyche he says: "Only on one side is it something that has come to be, and, as such subject to the causal standpoint. The other side is in the process of becoming, and can only be grasped synthetically or constructively. The causal standpoint merely inquires how this psyche has become what it is, as we see it today. The constructive standpoint asks how, out of this present psyche, a bridge can be built into its own future."[11]

Amplification, the bringing of historical and cultural associations to bear on unconscious processes for the purpose of illuminating the deeper roots at play, became one of Jung's key methods. He used this to identify and initiate a relationship with the archetypal contents constellating in his work with patients. The network qualities of these associational grids will be examined later in this chapter. Conceptually and practically, Jung was working within a holistic paradigm at least from the time of his break with Freud on. To better contextualize this, we turn to the history of holism within science.

## *Holism in Science, Field Theory*

While traditional cultures have often viewed their entire world as alive and profoundly interconnected in mysterious, magical ways, frequently portrayed in their mythologies, these notions are usually dismissed and omitted from the history of science as mere superstitions. However, in the last half century the way in which the history of science itself has been constructed is under investigation by scholars, and alternative views are emerging. As an example among the growing number of scholars in this field, the works of Betty Jo Teeter Dobbs[12] on Sir Isaac Newton's interest in alchemy have been groundbreaking. In a particularly relevant study for this essay, Val Dusek, a philosopher of science at the University of New Hampshire with no stated interest in Jung (he only mentions Jung in reference to Pauli, on page 162), offers a detailed historical argument for holistic influences on the formulation, development, and implementation of electromagnetic field theory, what is often referred to as classical field theory in his 1999 book, *The Holistic Inspirations of Physics*. Dusek identifies three worldviews as having links, either directly or indirectly, to classical field theory: traditional Chinese thought, Renaissance hermetic or occult theory, and German Romantic philosophy. Students of Jung will immediately recognize the relevance of all of these systems to Jung's psychological theories, including synchronicity; they would include his interest in texts such as the *I Ching* and *The Secret of the Golden Flower*, many of his sources for his alchemical writing, as well as the philosophical roots of much of depth psychology in nineteenth-century German philosophy and literature. Thus a closer look at field theory as informing the scientific views of the world during Jung's life will assist us in assessing its relevance in his theories, especially of synchronicity.

To locate the development of classical field theory, itself a nineteenth-century achievement, in the history of scientific ideas, a bit of background will help. As I have briefly written elsewhere,[13] the origins of modern science are usually placed in the seventeenth century, though even orthodox histories of science recognize a few significant individuals prior to this, most notably Copernicus (1473–1543), and several others whose lives spanned into the seventeenth century: Tycho Brahe (1546–1601), Galileo (1564–1642), and Kepler (1571–1630) who, as seen in chapter 1, was a subject of great interest to Pauli ("The Influence of Archetypal Ideas on the Scientific Theories of Kepler"). Those who articulated basic, universal laws of physics, especially when stated in mathematical terms, are generally heralded as the founders of the Western scientific view of the cosmos. Although Kepler did begin this quantification of nature, albeit in a heuristic manner, with his laws of planetary motion, it was without a deeper explanatory theory that would have provided a rationale for the observations and testable hypotheses to extend them. Thus the philosopher-scientist-mathematicians who sought to both systematize and explain natural phenomenon are given pride of place, beginning with René Descartes with his analytical geometry. Descartes is also known for his philosophical views stemming from his meditations, especially the view of soul as wholly separate from the body, a radical dualism in which matter and mind are completely distinct entities. Centuries of debate on the origins and nature of consciousness began with Descartes; this problem is (re)gaining attention in the twenty-first century as technological probing of the brain/mind interplay is becoming accessible to scientific exploration.

The greatest exponent of the mathematical approach during this inaugural period was, of course, Isaac Newton. Using his laws of motion combined with his conception of universal gravitation, Newton was able to give an accurate theoretical account for Kepler's observational "laws" of planetary motion. The subsequent success of Newtonian physics resulted in a mechanistic worldview that held sway for several centuries and still has application for human scale observations, but this achievement was troubled over time on two major points. First, an understanding of gravity: while Newton's laws gave accurate mathematical description of gravitational forces and the movement of bodies, especially observable celestial objects like planets and moons, the means by which this force was transmitted remained uncomfortably mysterious, being formulated as action at a distance. Second, the model implicitly held space to be empty and absolute, a three-dimensional Cartesian framework through which bodies moved. Time was likewise seen in *absolute* terms, a constant one way flow from past through the present to the future that could be arbitrarily subdivided into units using mechanical devices such as clocks. This view of absolute time and space would be severely challenged as an accurate description of reality in the early twentieth century.

As recent biographers of the scientists of the sixteenth and seventeenth centuries have taught us, the lives of these figures were more complex than can be derived from their scientific accomplishments. The holistic traditions were not dissociated from their thinking. Newton himself wrote far more on alchemy than on mathematical physics. Leibniz, the codiscoverer of calculus alongside Newton, was deeply concerned about symbolic thought—for him mathematics was part of a search for a universal language, and he has been firmly placed within the hermetic tradition by Frances Yates.[14] Most of the scientists and mathematicians of the period had strong philosophical interests that went well beyond the bounds of what could be quantified, but these views were edited out of the subsequent Enlightenment's reductionistic reading of nature.

While there were many challenges to the reductive views, their explanatory power has been very persuasive, and they have persisted into the contemporary world, though increasingly recognized as valid only for select situations and specific conditions. Some of the most serious criticism initially came from philosophers starting in the seventeenth century. Leibniz with his attention to the continuum (a sort of pleromatic background to the universe, a holistic fundament) opposed the atomistic view of Newtonian particulate bodies, he also presented perspectives linking time and space as being relational— the later caused Einstein to declare himself a "Leibnizian"[15]—rejecting Newton's absolutes of time and space. For Leibniz matter consisted of intensifications of forces or energy as dimensionless points in the continuum, expressions of monads. While details of Leibniz's theory of monads is beyond the scope of this chapter, it included the notion of a preestablished harmony among monads that, as noted in chapter 1, served as one of the key precursors to Jung's idea of synchronicity. For Leibniz each monad is as if a mirror in which all of the universe/ all other monads is reflected. Similarly, Spinoza in rejecting Descartes' dualism developed his dual-aspect monism (mind and matter are two different aspects of an underlying unity, a radically holistic stance). Strikingly, this last theory has recently enjoyed resurgence among some neuroscientists examining the brain/mind interface.[16] Similarly, Leibniz's ideas as reworked by Jung might also shed important light on the mind-body problem.[17]

By the end of the eighteenth century reactions to "Enlightenment" science had set in, especially in Germanic culture. Guided by Kant's series of critiques, German Romanticism and Classicism revived interest in Spinoza through various figures, including Goethe and Schelling with his *Naturphilosopie*. Alternative, process-oriented ways of envisioning and conducting science were suggested. Although at the time these approaches had few successes and quickly became marginalized, there was one area of importance to our theme, the discovery of the link between electricity and magnetism in 1820 by Hans Christian Oersted, who had studied with German idealist philosopher Johann Gottlieb Fichte. The observation was made serendipitously in a classroom demonstration when Oersted noticed a compass needle responding to a current passing through a nearby wire. Although his theory about this was not well developed, this observation served as a spur to the great British experimentalist Michael Faraday.

From a modest background, Faraday lacked a mathematical education but was brilliant in the laboratory. In his study of electrical and magnetic phenomena he identified lines of forces, for example, seeing magnetic strain as permeating the space around magnetic phenomena (fig. 2), he identified the circularity of the force and its persistence in a vacuum, that it was nonlinear and impacted space itself without a particulate medium. He developed this into the idea of a field, first presented in June 1845 at a meeting of the British Association for the Advancement of Science,[18] and went on to articulate field theory more generally. Rejecting Newtonian views of space as empty and absolute,

Faraday instead envisioned the space around electric and magnetic phenomena as permeated, even composed of lines of electromagnetic force, and in a great intuitive leap he suggested that these lines of force could carry the "ray vibrations of light." He also saw that analogous lines of force could account for gravitation, thus in one stroke producing a theory for the propagation of light and gravity, questioning the notion of absolute space and dismissing action at a distance. This was the greatest intellectual breakthrough in understanding of the physical world since Newton. From a Jungian perspective we would identify this as the reemergence of an archetypal idea leading to a vision of a wholly interconnected universe, an image that Jung would draw upon.

Faraday was also devoutly religious, an active member of the Sandemanian sect. This was a small Scottish group who strictly adhered to the Bible in literalistic fashion. Faraday's biographers (Cantor and colleagues) cite a number of points on which his religious beliefs positively impacted his views of science. These include his search for a conserved relationship between electricity and magnetism; he believed that the total amount of force should remain constant and unchanging, though its expressed forms may alter—a scientific error as it is energy that is conserved, not force. However, his belief in conservation based on religious grounds did successfully lead him to his law of electromagnetic induction, directly linking electromotive force (current flow) with magnetic flux (varying magnetic field), uniting phenomena that had been treated previously as unrelated. Field theory comes directly out of envisioning the interrelations of lines of force, which draws upon both scientific observation and religious conviction. Thus we have further evidence that an archetypal pattern has constellated and is emerging in this new paradigm.

In 1857, after much frustration in trying to convince his fellow scientists and engineers of the validity of field theory, Faraday sent a copy of his paper on conservation of force to a young James Clerk Maxwell. In a long letter of supportive response, Maxwell evokes an archetypal image: "your lines of force can 'weave a web across the sky' and lead the stars in their courses without any necessarily immediate connection with the objects of their attraction."[19] By this time,

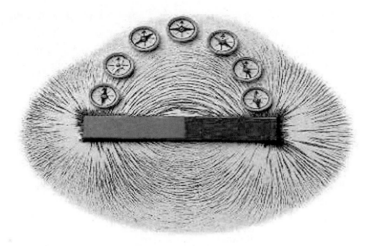

*Figure 2. Magnetic lines of force.*

Maxwell himself had already become enthusiastic about Faraday's ideas, having read several papers on Faraday's lines of force in 1855 and 1856 to the Cambridge Philosophical Society.

Within the limits of classical physics Faraday's insights were brought to their fullest expression by James Clerk Maxwell from 1862 to 1865. Among his numerous, brilliant achievements, Maxwell worked out a complete, rigorous mathematical expression for the electromagnetic field, not only providing the equations that unify electric and magnetic phenomena but also demonstrating that light was a form of electromagnetic radiation with a spectral range extending far beyond visible light in both directions—the ultraviolet and infrared ends of the visible spectrum. This model of course later supplied Jung with his apt metaphor for archetypal processes having both spiritual and instinctual dimensions. Newtonian notions of absolute space and time as well as action at a distance were now irrefutably overturned.

The parallels between the study of electromagnetism in nineteenth-century science and the fascination with hypnotic phenomena often referred to as a form of "magnetism" can only be noted in passing, but they do link directly to the intense interest at the time in mediums, as in William James's study of Leonora Piper and in Jung's medical dissertation where he reports his observation on his cousin, a medium, and refers to "magnetic passes." One potential area for further exploration in this realm would be to look more closely at Jung's notion of the "psychoid" in a comparison with studies in contemporary neuroscience, for example with transcranial magnetic stimulation—a technique employing changing magnetic fields to induce temporary (nondestructive) virtual lesions in the brain, which can be helpful in studying the functionality of various loci as well as examining connectivity of neuronal groups for their impact on consciousness, among other things.

In a surprisingly brief time Maxwell's own work was used as a springboard for a much more radical revision of physics through field theory. In 1905 Einstein produced four major papers, including his article "On the Electrodynamics of Moving Bodies," which proposed his special theory of relativity (the relativity of all inertial frames of reference). By 1915–16 Einstein had articulated his general theory of relativity, unifying special relativity, Newton's universal gravitation with a new, and non-Euclidian geometric view of space-time—gravitational acceleration arises from the curvature of space-time by the mass-energy and momentum content of matter.[20] This in turn had a profound impact on psychological theorizing.

Field theories generally are derived from studying interactions; whatever discipline uses such a theory, its application focuses on manifestations or expressions of an underlying connecting principle. As traced above, during the period from the 1870s well into the twentieth century, field theories were defining the Zeitgeist, especially in the physical sciences, and were being imported into psychology by notable figures such as William James with his "field of consciousness."[21] Jung found much inspiration in James's ideas and, as mentioned in chapter 1, Jung had had Einstein, the greatest field theorist of the twentieth century, to his house as a dinner guest on several occasions during the period, recall: "when Einstein was developing his first theory of relativity . . . It was Einstein who first started me off thinking about a possible relativity of time as well as space, and their psychic conditionality."[22] Although Jung does not explicitly refer to his model of the psyche as a form of field theory, it clearly owes much to this formulation. Nevertheless, his understanding of such theories tended to be more classical than modern. Gieser points out how Pauli was unconvinced by Jung's views of an objective psyche, she writes:

> Jung's assumption that the unconscious contains autonomous, regular processes that are *unrelated* to consciousness was epistemologically unacceptable to Pauli. It reminded him of the antiquated viewpoint of classical physics that one can describe the objective order in the cosmos without taking the moment of observation . . . into account. Pauli labelled this position "the classical idea of the objective reality of the cosmos." He compared Jung's way of describing the unconscious with the classical field concepts of physics and Maxwell's equations. Jung still used a mode of description which did not take the new epistemological situation revealed by quantum physics satisfactorily into account. Despite many advances in that direction he still had a tendency to treat the unconscious as a field that may be observed without considering the influence of the observation.[23]

The full measure of this critique has not yet been taken. The recent employment of emergentist models to Jung's theories forms an attempt to rectify such concerns; the success of this endeavor, which this text partakes in, remains uncertain as yet.

By moving to a field model Jung's view of the archetypes of the collective unconscious can be reformulated. Each archetype can be seen as a node embedded within the larger context of a polycentric whole, with sets of links or connections weaving the archetypes into a network that, as I have suggested elsewhere, has scale-free properties.[24] Then in terms of psychodynamics, Jung's 1946 monograph, "Psychology of the Transference," presents an interactive field model emerging from a background archetypal field. The scientific investigations of field theory in physics in relation to holistic perspectives has continued most notably in the work of David Bohm and his students such as David Peat (who has written on synchronicity) on what they term the "implicate order."

That these field descriptions derive from archetypal fantasies can be seen through amplification. The *unus mundus* of alchemy is one example of a unified field. Another archetypal field image is "Indra's net" from Indian and Chinese Buddhist philosophy. This image is one of the primary metaphors of the Hua-yen, or flower garland school:

> In the heaven of the great god Indra is said to be a vast and shimmering net, finer than a spider's web, stretching to the outermost reaches of space. Strung at each intersection of its diaphanous threads is a reflecting jewel. Since the net is infinite in extent, the jewels are infinite in number. In the glistening surface of each jewel is reflected all the other jewels, even those in the furthest corner of the heavens. In each reflection, again are reflected all the infinitely many other jewels, so that by this process, reflections of reflections continue without end.[25]

As already seen, Leibniz's monads also share this same fundamental image, his mirror thesis insists that each monad reflects all others, that is, the whole universe in itself. A holistic, radically interconnected, reflective universe has been a recurrent imagining of humanity, and Jung's theory of the Self together with the collective unconscious offer a psychological reading of this archetypal pattern. Synchronicity becomes a particularly potent manifestation of the field with the resonant reflections of internal and external events.

In the next chapter we will examine a contemporary form of scientific holism. Applying theories that have been gaining widespread acceptance in various disciplines will offer the opportunity of updating and reevaluating some of Jung's key concepts.

## CHAPTER 3

# Complexity, Emergence, and Symmetry

## The New Science of Complexity and Emergence

Several streams of research have converged over the past half century to create a new way of looking at phenomena that had been too difficult to assess with previous scientific models. With the advent of high-speed computers readily accessible to researchers, problems that had previously been unassailable began to yield to computer modeling. Solutions were not based on single, unambiguous mathematical "answers" but were approached by optimizing the fit between models and observations on real systems. Additionally, it became possible to analyze systems operating far from equilibrium, systems that interacted with their environments and had spontaneous, adaptive responses. The systems of interest display complexity, that is, they have emergent properties, meaning that interactions among the parts produce behaviors that are greater than the sum of the interactions but also manifest new, unexpected higher levels of functioning and order in the process of adapting to their surroundings. I have traced some of these ideas in other publications with applications to Jungian psychology.[1] In their macrobehaviors complex adaptive systems (CAS) with emergent properties display holistic features.[2]

The return of holism in the sciences through complexity theory has cut across traditional academic disciplines. The emergentist paradigm appears to have applicability at all levels of scale from the most microscopic/subatomic descriptions of physics, on through aggregate phenomena in chemistry, biology, and astronomy, as well as in the human and social sciences. Not only is it useful in explaining the way complex systems operate at all these levels, but it also appears to be integral in our understanding of the transitions between levels. Perhaps one of the most relevant examples is the emergence of mind from the body/brain matrix. Thus philosophy and psychology have also come to value the insights that can be derived from employing complexity theory.

To give a bit fuller picture, complex systems are nonlinear, so that seemingly minor alterations in initial conditions, can result in surprisingly large changes, for example, the famous "butterfly effect" first noted in applying chaos theory to weather systems.[3] CAS are distinct for their self-organizing properties; new levels of organization come at the expense of dissipation of energy. As mentioned, such systems operate far from equilibrium and so cannot be analyzed by the classical laws of thermodynamics. The last point can serve as a starting place for reconsideration of Jung's formulation of synchronicity in terms of emergence.[4] In his synchronicity essay Jung saw meaningful coincidence as being inexplicable and acausal because for him they lay outside of energetic phenomena. With access to complexity theory, this can be reconsidered in the light of the energetics of open systems far from equilibrium, capable of developing CAS. Such a perspective was unfortunately in its infancy at the time Jung was writing his essay on synchronicity and thus not available for his consideration.

The higher order phenomena associated with the self-organizing features of CAS, that is, emergence, tends to appear at the edge of order and chaos. This seems a remarkably useful way of describing and tracking Jungian analytic process—a suggested nosology, organizing a set of clinical observations based on this formulation, has been presented (see Cambray, "Synchronicity and Emergence," 419–31). In terms of field theory, emergent phenomena would be expected to occur in just those regions of the field that are undergoing self-organization. It may be helpful to provide some examples.

One of the more striking entomological examples of self-organization with a powerful adaptive outcome was noted by Diane Martindale in *Scientific American:*

Hundreds of the parasitic tiny blister beetle larvae clump together to mimic the shape and color of a female bee. When an amorous male bee attempts to mate, the beetle larvae grab his chest hair and are carried off. Then, when the duped male mates with a real female bee, the larvae transfer to her back and ride off to the nest, where they help themselves to pollen. The cooperative behavior of the beetle larvae had been virtually unknown in the insect world except among social species such as bees and ants. The report also notes that beetle larvae clumps must also smell like female bees, because painted models do not fool the male bee. (Martindale, "Beetle to Bee")

To complete their life cycle the beetle larvae must ingest the pollen, so that the emergent "bee-ing" they form is critical to their survival as a species. It should be noted that given the limited neuronal resources of the larvae there is no possibility of their harboring an internal image of the bee, they simply do not have the physiology to support this as an internal structure. There are many other insect examples available, to cite just a couple: the behavior of termite colonies (a classic study by Eugene Marais first published a year after his death in 1936, *The Soul of the White Ant* [1971], is known to many Jungians); the coordinated synchronous flashing in a nocturnal mating display of tens of thousands of Malaysian fireflies so that whole trees light up and flash "on and off"—this synchronization is accomplished without any leader or external coordinating cues and is based solely on local interactions.[5]

The manner in which insects communicate and can collectively act to produce purposeful, adaptive behaviors has long fascinated depth psychologists. In several passages referring to telepathy Freud makes the link explicit:

It is a familiar fact that we do not know how the common purpose comes about in the great insect communities: possibly it is done by means of a direct psychical transference of this kind. One is led to a suspicion that this is the original, archaic method of communication between individuals and that in the course of phylogenetic evolution it has been replaced by the better method of giving information with the help of signals which are picked up by the sense organs. But the older method might have persisted in the background and still be able to put itself into effect under certain conditions—for instance, in passionately excited mobs.[6]

Freud goes on in the next paragraph to extend this mechanism to children:

> If there is such a thing as telepathy as a real process, we may suspect that, in spite of its being so hard to demonstrate, it is quite a common phenomenon. It would tally with our expectations if we were able to point to it particularly in the mental life of children. Here we are reminded of the frequent anxiety felt by children over the idea that their parents know all their thoughts.[7]

Similarly, Jung was drawn to insect examples for synchronicity (the famous Scarabaeid beetle story) and for explicating his archetype theory (the leaf-cutting ant and yucca moth examples he borrowed from Conway Lloyd Morgan's *Habit and Instinct*, see Hogenson, "The Baldwin Effect," for details). Perhaps this interest of the founders in insects and mental life resides in an intuition that there have been two major approaches in evolution to the development of intention and purpose: collective behaviors requiring rapid communication between organisms, while relying on self-organizing properties of collective systems and alternatively an internalization of separate units to reside in a single individual who would also retain, à la Freud, vestiges of this other communication system—the human brain with its roughly hundred billion neurons being a relevant example.

Jung's notion of the Self also can be read as an emergent property of the psyche, and as I've previously shown synchronicity is consistent with an emergentist paradigm. In recent years growing numbers of analytical psychologists have begun to apply systems and complexity theories to the Jungian approach. In addition to the Hogenson paper already mentioned, a few other authors whose writings have appeared in the *Journal of Analytical Psychology* over the last several years with an explicit focus on these theories include: the inaugural work of David Tresan, and an important contribution by Peter Saunders and Patricia Skar, and Jean Knox, Margaret Wilkinson, Maxson McDowell, François Martin-Vallas, and Hester Solomon;[8] it is implicit in the work of many others. Most of the authors in the volume I coedited with Linda Carter[9] also employed this approach; a recent IAAP International Congress in Barcelona, "Edges of Experience: Memory and Emergence"[10] resulted in many papers devoted to the application of emergence theory. The recognition of emergent phenomena in the cognitive and neurosciences, attachment, psychoanalytic and consciousness studies, as well as in the more traditional sciences makes its inclusion within the Jungian literature especially important in keeping analytical psychology relevant.

Nonanalytic writers, including philosophers of mind, are drawn to emergence because of its significance for transcendence, ultimately linking the scientific and the spiritual.[11] Emergence of levels beyond that of the individual mind is key in this, and collective intelligence of various sorts, such as produced by cultures, point to this (for a popular study on collective intelligence see Surowiecki's *The Wisdom of Crowds*). A discussion of a few of these transindividual relationships will be highlighted in chapter 4.

Dynamic networks, composed of things and/or processes that are interconnected, make up a particularly interesting and relevant subset of CAS. These networks tend to be described in terms of "hubs," centers that are richly linked to other centers, and "nodes" that have lesser numbers of links. Mapping the hyperlinks between various sites of the World Wide Web was one of the systems that gave rise to this description; perhaps more familiar are the maps of airlines' connections found in the seat pocket of most commercial airlines; these maps show the major cities the company flies to as hubs, along with smaller cities and towns less richly linked, the nodes. An essential feature of these networks is their "scale-free" properties, that is, they are fractal-like, appearing similar at various levels of scale. Many natural systems display self-similarity at several scales, for example, fern fronds, river systems, the branching of nerves, blood vessels, mountain ranges, and so on. Significantly, scale-free networks are known to have self-organizing properties.

A transpersonal psyche with a collective unconscious composed of the sum of all of the archetypes as Jung's model proposed would have features of a scale-free network structure. His methodology for approaching the unconscious, especially amplification, similarly can be seen to map and understand the psyche as such a network, as I have detailed elsewhere.[12] The early presentations of Jung's model, as by Jacobi,[13] offered an association grid that is probably too regular and rigid in form but captures the polycentric network aspect of the model (fig. 3). In the second generation of Jungians, a relaxing of the network grid can be found most directly in Edinger's *Anatomy of the Psyche*,[14] with its alchemical amplificatory maps at the start of each chapter (fig. 4). Another feature of scale-free networks enters more subtly in Edinger's diagrams, looking at the connecting lines there is an implicit suggestion of variable strengths of the associational links. The importance of weak links in stabilizing complex systems as well as providing them with increased flexibility is an area scientists are currently researching.[15]

*Figure 3. Jacobi's dream elements network. Reproduced from Jolande Jacobi (1973), The Psychology of C. G. Jung. Yale University Press, p. 87.*

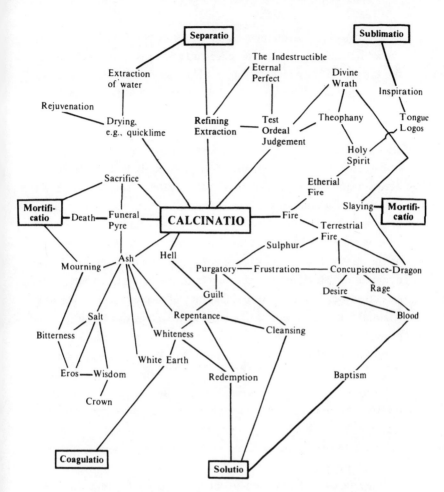

*Figure 4. Edinger's association network. Reprinted by permission of Open Court Publishing Company, a division of Carus Publishing Company, Peru, Ill., from* Anatomy of the Psyche *by Edward Edinger, copyright © 1985 by Open Court Publishing Company.*

As the current generation of Jungians study and incorporate these models into analytic theory, a full formulation of a psychological network model probably could assist in broadly integrating psychoanalytic models into a holistic one. The personal complexes residual from childhood would be seen as organized around the major archetypes active during early development; these would form the hubs of analytic theory. The interactive patterns of object relations including those that inform the transference/countertransference field reveal the interconnections between hubs. Then as individuation proceeds out of childhood, through the socially adaptive period of young adulthood and adult life (Jung's "first half of life") toward the psychological challenges of maturity and old age (whether of the whole personality or particular aspects of development), the archetypal patterns active also shift away from the more commonly trodden pathways between hubs, to explorations of nodal patterns and their linkages that are on the margins. These elements on the margins may have previously been left unexplored by the person through inattention, lack of readiness to engage them, or various defensive maneuvers, of the ego or the Self, placing them in the "shadow" region of the dynamic unconscious. As experiences in life bring us to uncharted aspects of our being, often revealed only after previous unconscious encumbrances have been worked through, we may then explore these nodes. Integration of the potentials held in these positions in turn fosters individuation. A clinical example of this type of process was discussed in a recent essay of mine based on a dream in which a man in his mid-thirties is going through a set of life changes: "I have come for my session. I'm about to ring your bell and enter when I look up. The light is changing. It is twilight and the stars are coming out. I'm surprised to see a constellation that I've never seen before. It is new and it is nearly overhead."[16]

The new constellation, a new pattern of psychological being, held previously unused aspects of the personality that were essential for the therapeutic work to proceed, more details can be found in that essay.

## Symmetry

Scientific studies across a variety of disciplines have revealed the importance of symmetry in relation to complexity. The primary observation is that the formation of, or increase in, complexity is characterized by a breaking of the symmetry of the precursor state.[17] To better understand the significance of breaking symmetry and how this is relevant to the topic under discussion, a brief discussion of symmetry may be useful.

Nontechnical definitions of symmetry tend to emphasize the aesthetic feeling associated with it, for example, "beauty of form arising from balanced proportions."[18] The etymology can be traced back to the Greek, ςυμ (sym)—"together"/"with"; and μετρον (metron)—"measure"/"standard"; combining to make ςυμμετρια (symmetria)—"symmetry"/"due proportion"/"commensurate," as can be found in Euclid's elements. According to the Stanford Encyclopedia of Philosophy,

> it quickly acquired a further, more general, meaning: that of a proportion relation, grounded on (integer) numbers, and with the function of harmonizing the different elements into a unitary whole. From the outset, then, symmetry was closely related to harmony, beauty and unity. . . . [A] different notion of symmetry emerged in the seventeenth century, grounded not on proportions but on an equality relation between elements that are opposed, such as the left and right parts of a figure. Crucially, the parts are interchangeable with respect to the whole.[19]

Although symmetry was to gradually enter into scientific discourse, with great advances being made in mathematics during the second half of the nineteenth century with the theory of groups, up until the twentieth century utilization of symmetry was most prevalent in the arts. The expressions of forms, whether in painting, architecture, poetry, dance, or music drew upon symmetrical features—note that for the last three this can occur in time as well as in space. In fact, links between various arts were often made through identifying symmetrical patterns in common. For example, much of Bach's music has an associated architectural feeling that comes in part from constructions based on symmetrical phrases arranged into a hierarchy of components capable of expressing diversity within the overall composition. Goethe is often quoted as remarking, "I call architecture frozen music."[20]

There are numerous kinds of symmetries, such as bilateral or mirror symmetry (our two hands or our faces in a limited approximation exhibit this—while you cannot rotate one hand to match the other, they do have a mirror image relationship), or radial/rotational symmetry (arranged around a center point in which a partial turn restores the original figure unchanged, as some mandalas do). In general, a characteristic feature of a symmetrical relationship is invariance or equivalence, that is, parts of an object are equivalent to one another in a symmetry operation; they can be interchanged through the symmetry operation leaving the whole object unchanged, or invariant.

The human mind's capacity to use symmetry unconsciously can be striking. The visual neuroscientist V. S. Ramachandran has published studies in which he and his team were able to relieve phantom limb discomfort (a felt sense of painful paralysis often experienced after the amputation of a limb) through the use of mirror symmetry. In brief, Ramachandran reports:

> We propped up a mirror vertically on a table in front of a prone patient, so that it was at right angles to his chest, and asked him to position his paralyzed phantom left arm on the left of the mirror and mimic its posture with his right hand, which was on the right side of the mirror. We then asked him to look into the right-hand side of the mirror so that he saw the mirror reflection of his intact hand optically superimposed on the felt location of the phantom. We then asked him to try to make symmetrical movements of both hands, such as clapping or conducting an orchestra, while looking in the mirror. Imagine his amazement and ours when suddenly he not only saw the phantom move but felt it move as well. . . . Many patients have found that this sudden sense of voluntary control and movement in the phantom produces relief from the spasm or awkward posture that was causing much of the agonizing pain in the phantom.[21]

His group has gone on to extend pain relief to other syndromes and has speculated about brain mechanisms that might underlie some forms of transsexual body imagery.

In a completely separate set of studies, Thornhill and Gangestad have explored how aesthetic preferences in human sexual relations have physiological aspects based on hormones and symmetry, though obviously these are not the only factors operating in these aesthetic judgments. There seems to be a sex-specific evolutionary adaptive application of symmetrical features. In particular, they note:

> The body scent of men who have greater body bilateral symmetry is rated as more attractive by normally ovulating (non-pill-using) women during the period of highest fertility . . . within the menstrual cycle. Women in low-fertility phases of the cycle and women using hormone-based contraceptives do not show this pattern. . . . The current study also examined women's scent attractiveness to men and found no evidence that men prefer the scent of symmetric women. We propose that the scent of symmetry is an honest signal of phenotypic and genetic quality in the human male. . . . The results overall suggest that women have an evolved preference for sires with good genes.[22]

Thornhill, Gangestad, and Comer have also shown that "mates of symmetrical men show the most reported copulatory orgasms,"[23] to which they give the evolutionarily adaptive advantage of increasing sperm retention. They have also looked at the role of symmetry in various secondary sexual characteristics, but this is beyond the scope of this chapter. From an evolutionary perspective there have also been studies exploring links between bilateral symmetry and long-term health; deviations from symmetry due to various sources such as genetic problems or environmental and developmental stresses may be unconsciously detected by potential mates. Although these results are relatively new, it is clear that symmetry has an important role in erotic life, operating at conscious, preconscious, and unconscious levels of the psyche. As more data are accumulated it will probably be productive to reflect and speculate on how various elements of the analytic situation play upon this link, such as couch versus face-to-face encounters.

Returning to the basics of symmetry, simple objects tend to have high degrees of symmetry. Consider a perfect circle: you can rotate the circle around its midpoint any number of degrees and the resulting image would remain unchanged (radial symmetry); you can also place a (straight) mirror across it at any point and so long as it goes through the center, the half circle in the mirror plus the half circle you see in front of the mirror allows you to continue to see the whole circle unchanged. With an equilateral triangle or a square there is less symmetry; rotations and reflections (all through the midpoint) are in multiples of 90 degrees for the square or 120 degrees for the triangle. High degrees of symmetry can be obtained from two opposing directions: (1) very ordered structures like crystal lattices; (2) complete randomization (chaos), so that an equal, homogenous distribution is obtained in all directions, as in an inert gas.

If we look at a more complex object such as a Celtic knot (fig. 5), we can see that a mirror through either of the central axes will not create an equivalent structure; only a rotation about the central point of 180 degrees perpendicular to the image will give an invariant form (rotations of 180 degrees through either of the in-plane axes will require an additional rotation through the other axis or a mirror reflection to remain invariant).

In the Islamic world iconographic art is generally forbidden, so elaborate use of symmetric patterns is often used for decorative purposes that simultaneously evoke a spiritual feeling. For plane surfaces (those in two dimensions) mathematicians have proven there are only seventeen basic symmetry patterns possible; the Alhambra

*Figure 5. Celtic knot.*

in Granada, southern Spain, from the period of Muslim rule (Nasrid kingdom) displays all seventeen patterns—the tile patterns from the Alhambra were influential on the twentieth century's premier artist of symmetry, M. C. Escher.[24]

A third common form of symmetry is translational symmetry. This occurs when an object or pattern is repeated using the same motion a number of times. Railroad tracks are an easily visualized form of translation symmetry. Escher is renowned for his works that exhibit a particularly complex form of translational symmetry, the glide-reflectional symmetry, for some examples see the Web site http://www.mcescher.com/.[25] For those who study symmetry these figures have translational symmetries in numerous directions, plus various reflective and rotational symmetries. Recently, scientists have been looking at medieval Islamic buildings, realizing that tile patterns demonstrate remarkable mathematical understandings and break-throughs not found in the West until the last half of the twentieth century. One example that has received significant press coverage is a highly complex multilevel pattern found in a fifteenth-century shrine in Isfahan, Iran. The interlocking tiles are arranged in a man-ner so that the pattern never repeats, though there are recognizable repeating subpatterns; these are known by mathematicians as "quasi crystals."[26]

## Symmetry and Emergence

The field theories discussed in the previous chapter all exhibit signifi-cant symmetry in terms of laws of nature, and especially in time—a new form of symmetry not fully recognized prior to modernity. However, with the advent of dynamic quantum theory and studies in high-energy physics, some shocking new results emerged. In 1956 two researchers at Columbia University, T. D. Lee and C. N. Yang, demon-strated in experiments with subatomic particles that parity (reflection symmetry) was not conserved in reactions involving "weak" nuclear forces (during beta decay).

The difficulty had already been set in motion when Paul Dirac combined Einstein's relativity with quantum mechanics and made the theoretical prediction of existence of antimatter in 1926. There was presumed to be a rigorous mirror relationship of antimatter to matter, a form of parity that was felt by physicists to be at the base of all laws of physics. When this was proven not to strictly hold for beta decay, it caused such a sensation that it made front-page news in the *New York Times*[27]; as republished in *Atom and Archetype*.[28] Wolfgang Pauli was one of the prominent physicists who was most stunned by this. Pauli at first could not accept the results: "I do not believe however that the Lord God is a WEAK left-hander."[29] In communications, Markus Fierz, twin brother of the Jungian analyst Heinrich Fierz, told Pauli that he (WP) had a "mirror complex,"[30] noting its appearance in his dreams as well as in his beliefs about physics. For Pauli the whole question of the relationship between physics and psychology "is that of a mirror image."[31] At first he attempted to seek a restoration of symmetry by going more deeply into the observations, "parity is restored when one takes into consideration enough of the variables characterizing the phenomenon (such as the 'CPT [charge, parity, and time] theorem . . .')."[32] But even this (CPT) has been called into question.

The attempt to restore symmetry becomes linked to synchronicity for Pauli, as when he writes Jung: "If the parapsychological phenomena go deeper, then the psyche has to be taken into consideration so as to be able to see the full symmetry of the phenomenon. . . . The question of 'how deep or how broad does one have to go to achieve full symmetry' ultimately seems to lead back to the problem—in your terminology—of the separation of the self from the ego."[33]

Pauli's speculations in turn provoke Jung to write his last personal letter to him.[34] Here is a selection of reflections from this letter:

a constellated, i.e., activated, archetype may not be the cause but is certainly a condition of synchronistic phenomena . . . occurrences might be expected that correspond to the archetype as a sort of mirror image . . . the physical problem of symmetry or asymmetry which coincides so oddly with my own preoccupation, is something analogous or parallel. Apart from the mirror image aspect of the phenomenon, the statements from the unconscious (represented by UFO legends, dreams, and images) point to a "slight left-handedness in God," in other words ... to a prevalence of the unconscious, expressed through "God's eyes."[35]

Jung then goes on to discuss the role of symbols in the individuation process, with the goal of wholeness, which he says

> should mean that the mirror-image effect, which dazzle us, would be removed ... this would be done by an "asymmetrical" Third, which prefers one direction; namely—according to legend— the direction toward greater differentiation of consciousness, as opposed to the balance of conscious-unconscious. . . . The parity operation corresponds to the psychological opposition. . . . The fact that it is precisely the weak interactions that exhibit asymmetry forms an almost comic parallel to the fact that it is precisely the infinitesimal, psychological factors, overlooked by all, that shake the foundations of our world.[36]

As he nears the end of this letter, Jung makes a statement that is of particular interest for this chapter. He says

> the psychoid archetype, where "psychic" and "material" are no longer viable as attributes or where the category of opposites becomes obsolete and every occurrence can only be asymmetrical; the reason for this is that an occurrence can only be the one or the other when it proceeds from an indistinguishable One.[37]

Thus in dialogue with Pauli, Jung moves beyond the bounds of symmetry, placing the deepest levels of psychological development as well as synchronicity in the realm of the asymmetric, coming through small seemingly insignificant breaks in symmetry. The furthest reaches of Jung's psychology can only be accessed through breaking symmetry, which we have seen is a way of complexification.

In this exchange with Pauli, I believe Jung is reaching his apogee in his understanding of the limits of symmetry. Jung's views of the Self give evidence of both his need for symmetrical ordering properties that tend to be associated with historical, aesthetic, and religious traditions, while also remaining open to the precarious, symmetry-breaking, emergent possibilities of the Self. By comparing the published diagrams in *Aion* with a previously unpublished initial drawing now at last in print—see Ann Lammers[38] and the letter of May 21, 1948 from Jung to Victor White[39]—a bold embrace of symmetry breaking by Jung can be clearly found.

To recapitulate: late in *Aion*, as Jung works his way through "Gnostic Symbols of the Self," he is at pains to represent the multidimensional quality of the Self through a set of geometric diagrams. Using a set of four octahedrons—double square pyramids (one of the Platonic solids)—each of which he has explicated as an elaboration of a quaternity at differing levels of being from inorganic matter (the Lapis Quaternio) up through images of the transcendental Self, the "higher Adam" (the Anthropos Quaternio), which he ultimately envisions in a set of nonlinear, circular processes (fig. 6). However, read in terms of emergence, these figures still retain a highly symmetric network, they are not free enough to manifest self-organizing features, even though that would be expected for manifestations of mind, including both individual and collective behaviors as well as the evolution of cultures that includes all of the highest aspirations of humans. Nevertheless, Jung's four "Quaternios" do attempt to offer a poetic expression of such knowledge in a highly compacted form. For a more detailed discussion of these levels from a classical Jungian perspective see Edinger's *The Aion Lectures*.[40]

In examining these figures composed of stacked octahedrons, it is evident that Jung was seeking a sufficiently complex way to present his evolving understanding of two thousand years of symbolism. His multidimensional geometric imaginings are closely linked with his attempt to break out of the trinitarian principles of religion and science as he understood it (for science it was space, time, causality) to express a Quaternitarian view that included "correspondence," that is, to his ideas about synchronicity.[41] These diagrams represent Jung's struggle to communicate a view of an archetypal Self in a manner that places it at the heart of emergent processes, it symbolizes the potential for emergence throughout the hierarchy of levels of being, from the mineral to the spirit. One striking feature in comparing these dia-

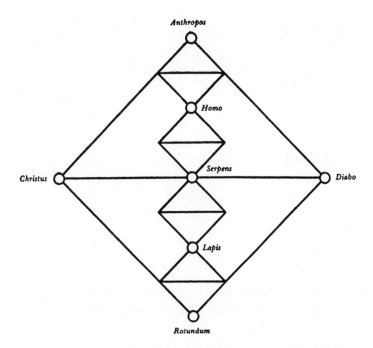

*Figure 6. Jung's image of the Self as four octahedrons. Reproduced from the*
Collected Works of C. G. Jung, *volume 9, part II,* Aion. *Princeton, N.J.:*
*Princeton/Bollengen, 1979 edition, p. 247. Permission from Paul & Peter Fritz AG*
*Literary Agency for the C. G. Jung Estate. Courtesy Stiftung der Werke von C. G. Jung.*

grams is the breaking of, or reduction in symmetry in Jung's fullest
representation, an image that remained unpublished until 2007.

In their general form Jung's diagrams all show highly regular, symmetric features; even the most complex of them demonstrates rotational as well mirror symmetry. However, unlike all of the diagrams
published in *Aion,* Jung's sketch to White (fig. 7) shows the top octahedron rotated 90 degrees relative to those below it and in the larger
diamond, diagonal lines linking the lower frontal face of the second
octahedron and with upper dorsal face of the third octahedron, which
reduces the symmetry of the whole figure to a single mirror plane.
Additionally, as noted by Lammers,[42] these diagonal lines, from matter to the ♂ symbol and mind (spirit) to the ♀ symbol, are omitted from the drawing in *Aion,* again simplifying and symmetrizing
the published figure relative to the one in the letter to White. This

lowering of symmetry suggests to me that this fullest expression of Jung's idea contains an impulse (I do not know if it was conscious or not) to break out of the excessive ordering that at times accompanied Jung's use of the Self (as with his own history of producing mandalas). The unacknowledged value in this diminishing of symmetry may be found in the increased complexity that results. Perhaps his need to remain open to the power of the numinous, which cannot always be reduced to symmetrical containment, informed his diagram to Victor White just as he spoke of his respect for various religious traditions as the closest approach he could come to faith[43]; it seems he needed a more complex view of the divine than he could find in traditional religion.

Although from a contemporary vantage point Jung's entire opus has an emergentist feeling to it, he built his theories without the benefit of the scientific findings on complexity which were not yet available during his lifetime. At times his view seemed too constrained by the longing for order that may have caused him to over-symmetrize his models, not unlike Einstein in his clinging to a static model of cosmology until it was evident that this was no longer viable, or his elusive search for a unified field theory.

## Symmetry Breaking and Synchronicity

For simple or linear systems (which can be complicated but are not complex in the sense of emergent properties) the whole is equal to the sum of its parts. In these, symmetric features are common and introduce redundancy into the pattern of the whole, so that one only needs a portion of the information in a linear system to construct the entire thing. The repetition of a pattern producing order tends to engender an aesthetic experience of beauty, which can of course have a calming effect on the mind, inducing a feeling of tranquility in resonance with the harmony of the symmetric form. The building up of symmetric forms is also crucial in early psychological development, hence the value of imitative learning (symmetrically internalizing the other, a root of empathy, which we will discuss at greater length in the next

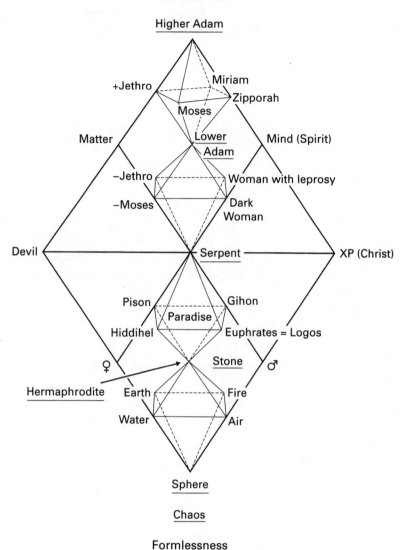

*Figure 7. Jung's image of the Self from a letter to Victor White. Permission from Paul & Peter Fritz AG Literary Agency for the C. G. Jung Estate. Courtesy Stiftung der Werke von C. G. Jung.*

chapter); and conversely it can even be a factor in erotic activation as already mentioned. However, in the generation of complex systems reduction in symmetry is integral to emergence.

In a truly complex system no single aspect has adequate information to represent the whole, nor can any single part statistically predict the dynamic behavior of the system, especially when it self-organizes. Symmetry is broken in what are called phase transitions, rapid, abrupt reorganizations in a dynamic system that radically restructure the system, allowing new forms to emerge.[44] Bearing the psychological equivalent of phase transitions and reorganizations can be highly stressful for an individual even if ultimately positive in transformative effect.

In the past half century spontaneous symmetry breaking has become recognized, not just as a disappointment to physicists seeking perfection, but also as a key to the existence of our cosmos. There are several extremely important spontaneous breaks in symmetry in the natural history of the world. The first has to due with the current model of the origins of our universe, the Big Bang discussed in chapter 1. As previously mentioned, once the initial explosion took place the universe appears to have expanded wholly randomly, i.e., no preferred direction; energy and matter were undifferentiated, in fact matter / antimatter pairs were in continuous creation/destruction. However, somewhere between $10^{-35}$ and $10^{-11}$ seconds after the Big Bang as the size of universe grew exponentially and the temperature fell there was a symmetry breaking phase transition in which matter came to predominate slightly over antimatter. This transition is the deep cause for why we live in a matter, rather than an antimatter universe (antimatter particles can be formed in the laboratory but are very short-lived due to joint annihilation when contact with matter is made; the matter/antimatter pairs are converted wholly into radiation).

The second relevant cosmic symmetry break, at least for life on earth, comes from the chemical history of our planet. Many biomolecules, the chemicals of life, have a distinct asymmetry about them. These molecules can exist in right- and left-handed forms, but one of the pair is usually biologically active and the other is inert. The separation and differentiation of molecules with these properties began in the nineteenth century. By 1811 crystals of quartz (a nonorganic mineral) were isolated exhibiting two forms having a mirror relationship and showing opposite optical properties.[45] Following this, none other than Louis Pasteur made the crucial studies, in 1848, on biological molecules. Pasteur used a microscope to separate crystals of sodium ammonium tartrate (isolated from wine), which were mirror images of one another (fig. 8). He then demonstrated that one form of the crystals when dissolved into a solution rotated the plane of polarized light to the right when such light was shown through the solution. Solutions of the mirror image form of the crystal rotated the plane of polarized light an equal but opposite direction, to the left. Pasteur thereby demonstrated that it was these molecules themselves that displayed handedness, not just the crystals; the molecules had an inherent chirality. Many different kinds of molecules isolated from biological systems have subsequently been shown to demonstrate a clear preference for "handedness," for example, left-handed amino acids (which are the building blocks of proteins and enzymes), and right-handed sugars; the opposite handed forms generally cannot be metabolized by earth-based life forms. In scientific language this preferred single-handedness is referred to as *homochirality;* nature clearly exhibits this, but the exact origins of this trait remain shrouded at present, though various theories have been postulated to try to explain how it first arose. Nevertheless, there was some selective pressure that produced this differentiation, a breaking of the symmetry associated with equal amounts of the precursor molecules in the prebiotic soup (an early form of this was called biopoesis, one of J. B. S. Haldane's ideas in the mid-1920s). This type of breaking of symmetry is a fundamental aspect of the origins of life.

Recall Jung's March 1959 letter to Erich Neumann, quoted in chapter 1, in which he suggested a psychoid aspect to synthesis that seemed to transcend ordinary natural laws during a period before consciousness had emerged. The original synthesis and selection of chiral molecules would certainly be a candidate for one of those synchronistic moments that would lie at the root of all living matter. Furthermore, in a parallel manner to such key biological processes, we might expect

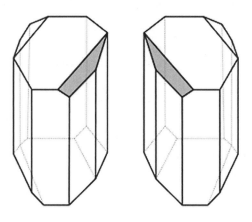

*Figure 8. Enantiomeric tartarate crystals.*

the origins and development of the mind to require symmetric and asymmetric components, with symmetry breaking as a key element in associated phase transitions.

The early mother-infant dyad often sustains a feeling of symmetric wholeness (oceanic states) that helps serve to contain the infant. In this vein psychoanalyst Thomas Ogden expanded on D. W. Winnicott's 1949 remark identifying the good-enough mother as one who tries to insulate her baby from coincidences, noting that "the coincidences or complications from which a baby needs to be insulated involve chance simultaneities of events that take place in the infant's internal and external realities at a time when the two are only beginning to be differentiated from one another."[46] However, for the child to develop a separate mind, a series of breaks in symmetry occur, around what we commonly think of as developmental milestones, which can be understood as phase transitions, most likely with concomitant neurophysiological changes, often with rapid onset. René Spitz in 1959 published a seminal monograph articulating early developmental steps occurring with concomitant psychological and neurobiological reorganization, such as the smile response. Classically, it has been the role of the father to function as an asymmetric third, to use Jung's terminology, to facilitate such transitions in a manner that is optimally disruptive rather than excessively so—to generate increased order through self-organization rather than dissolution into chaos. Obtaining the meaning from the psychoid dimension of such a process is where the symmetry-breaking aspect of synchronicity enters.

Finally, according to the Stanford Encyclopedia of Philosophy

> there is a close connection between symmetry and objectivity . . . the laws by means of which we describe the evolution of physical systems have an objective validity because they are the same for all observers . . . what is objective is what is invariant with respect to the transformation group of reference frames.[47]

By extension, events that are unique, not reproducible, and have an idiosyncratic quality are subjective, and subjectivity thus has an asymmetric dimension. Synchronicity is the study of such events where the meaningful experience of the person the event is happening to can be understood by others, as in the metaphoric resonances of the coincidence, but the unique quality of the experience cannot be wholly communicated. More deeply, grappling with the significance of a synchronistic experience will at some point require a differentiation, a breaking of the symmetry between inner and outer aspects of the event. The initial felt symmetry is a powerful inducement to attend to such events, but psychological development requires that we suffer awareness of the asymmetry—this I believe was what Jung was trying to communicate to Pauli about his "mirror complex," cited above.

## CHAPTER 4

# Empathy and
# the Analytic Field

The clinical utility and relevance of the topics in the previous chapters is not immediately self-evident; it requires some explicit reflection. Previously I have published a potential classification of synchronistic events occurring in psychotherapy based on a model from studies in self-organizing criticality.[1] In that paper I suggested that an examination of the intensities of synchronicities plotted against their frequencies could be explored. If a power law relationship between these variables were obtained, this would then indicate an underlying commonality of process across a range of synchronicities. As a first guess at intensities of such events, I drew up a qualitative scale based on clinical experience. These events can also be described in terms of emergent properties of field phenomena, and it is this aspect that will be explored in this chapter.

As a tool to help identify emergent events in an interactive field I will look at one form of resonant phenomena. In general, resonance indicates some form of attunement among elements or agents in a field; such interactions in turn can lead to emergent properties. The concept of resonance can readily be grasped in acoustic systems; consider a tuning fork used to tune a piano: striking the fork against a solid surface will set it vibrating at a specific frequency, producing a reference pitch; the relevant string on a piano can then be adjusted (tightened or loosened) so that the string resonates at the same frequency, so that the pitches match. In fact if the vibrating fork is put in proximity with the tuned string, this will then begin to vibrate with the same frequency—the two are said to be in resonance. All material things have vibrational potential; each has a natural frequency at which it vibrates, called a resonant frequency. If you put energy into the substance at its resonant frequency, it will vibrate or resonate correspondingly. One well-known example is the (opera) singer who can use his/her voice to shatter a glass by singing and holding a note that is at the resonant frequency of the glass; the glass begins to vibrate until it can no longer contain the vibratory movement and shatters to dissipate the energy. By analogy, we will look at resonance in psychological systems where the forms of emergence are more complex.

In the midst of his great treatise *Science and Civilization in China*, Joseph Needham tells a fifth-century CE anecdote of a Mr. Yin from Chinchow, who is reported to have asked a Taoist monk (Chang Yeh-Yuan), "What is really the fundamental idea (*thi*) of the Book of Changes (*I Ching*)?" To which the monk is said to have replied: "The fundamental idea of the *I Ching* can be expressed in one single word, Resonance (*kan*)."[2] Applied to the mind, ancient Taoists valued the original "empty" mind as that organ that can resonate most fully with nature. From a Jungian perspective this emptiness is not a dull blankness but a receptivity marked by nonattachment, with the releasing of prejudices and preconceptions, becoming open to archetypal possibilities. An experience of psychological depth can come from the resonance of this empty mind with the world, noting the impact, but not clinging to, the phenomena observed. From Jung's foreword to Richard Wilhelm's translation of the *I Ching* we know that he saw this oracular text as based on the principle that he termed *synchronicity*.[3] In the same vein both Lao Tzu and Chuang Tzu use the metaphor of a mirror for this state, for example, in *Chuang Tzu*, Book VII, we read: "When the perfect man employs his mind, it is a mirror. It conducts nothing and anticipates nothing."[4] Again in Book XIII he adds: "The still mind of the sage is the mirror of heaven and earth—the glass of all things."[5] For those who know Jung on the optimal mindset for approaching dreams, or later Wilfred Bion's ideas on entering the analytic field, a curiously familiar chord is sounded. The metaphor of the mirror is directly and intimately tied to mirror symmetry as discussed in the last chapter and will be expanded upon in this chapter.

The notion of a resonant, mirroring capacity of mind that can bring knowledge of our environment has a particular parallel in Western psychology that can be explored through the concept of *empathy*. The purpose is not to suggest an equivalency between empathy and the mind of the sage but rather to engage the evolving Western understanding of empathy in the hope that we may find intersections with Eastern attitudes on cultivating the mind that were helpful to Jung in his formulation of the synchronicity principle.

The articulated idea of empathy is of surprisingly recent vintage. The original term is German, *Einfühlung*, literally "feeling-into," coined by the art historian Robert Vischer only in 1873 and distinguished from an older notion, *Mitgefühl*, sympathy.[6] Vischer's work inaugurated the psychological approach to the study of aesthetics. His idea was to relate the dynamics within a work of art to the subjective experiences stemming from somatic and affective states engendered by viewing the art. Aesthetic pleasure was seen to be based in a melding of self and object, something he derived from the study of the projection of self in dreams. Vischer's *Einfühlung* thus involved an unconscious, involuntary act of transference of self into objects. All of this antedates Freud's psychoanalytic theorizing by twenty-five years. "Empathy" as the translation of *Einfühlung* entered the English language in 1909 through the work of the American psychologist Edward B. Titchener.[7]

The German philosopher of aesthetics, Theodor Lipps, in publications from 1900 to 1913 and beyond, further developed the psychological understanding of empathy by proposing the *inner imitation* of the actions of others as crucial for generating empathic experiences.[8] For Lipps human empathy included responses to gestures, facial expressions, and tone of voice, all carrying emotional qualities and capable of enlivening the same emotions in the viewer. However, Lipps also insisted that empathy is not an inference from analogy but a unique form of knowledge.

Both Jung and Freud derived their views on empathy directly from Lipps.[9] Jung equated Lipps's perspective to a central feature of the analytic process: "As a rule, the projection transfers unconscious contents into the object, for which reason *empathy is also termed 'trans-*

*ference*' in analytical psychology."[10] Although Jung does not write extensively about empathy as such, his ability to empathically enter into and grasp the psychological relevance of symbolic material was essential to his views of the psyche. After discussing some refinements in the understanding of empathy that have occurred since the early days of analysis, we will reexamine Jung's interactive field model as discussed in *The Psychology of the Transference,* with special attention to unconscious communications within analysis, in essence it offers a portrait of the archetypal field underlying empathy.

The clinical utility of an empathic stance toward patients and their unconscious processes, while recognized early on, has developed with increasing differentiation and valuing of the inner experience of the "other." As analytic theories and therapeutic methods probed into the origins of the sense of Self as well as the injuries and sufferings this is liable to, affective and interpersonal aspects at the core of the Self were identified. Over the last century modification of approaches to treatment have been proposed and debated. Sándor Ferenczi's active methods, H. S. Sullivan's interpersonal interviewing, Carl Rogers's client-centered therapy, among others but especially Heinz Kohut's "Self-Psychology" revision of analytic theory and practice employed empathy as primary means to enter into the interior world of the other. However, Kohut's formulation of empathy as vicarious introspection, or "the capacity to think and feel oneself into the inner life of another person"[11] relies heavily on the analyst's rational processing of his/her experience of the other while downplaying the immersive, affective components, including countertransference activations. Lest a skewed view of empathy come to prevail, a reassessment is in order; fortunately there are some new means of studying empathic phenomena.

## Neuroscience

In the last two decades the increasing sophistication of technical instrumentation and scientific formulations has opened new frontiers in exploring the neurobiological foundations of the mind. For most contemporary scientists and philosophers the phenomena of mind are neither reducible to neural processes nor wholly separate from somatic experience, but the mind is said to emerge from these in the sense of emergence as already discussed. The mind is conceptualized as being embedded in the body, and terms like *embodied cognition* are used to express the intimate and extensive involvement and interdependency of mental processes with those of somatic ones.

Uncovering and articulating details of the mind-body relationship is currently the subject of much intense research. An overlooked aspect of this relationship is the possible synchronistic dimension as discussed in chapter 1. Recall Jung's comment, "I must again stress the possibility that the relation between body and soul may yet be understood as a synchronistic one. Should this conjecture ever be proved, my present view that synchronicity is a relatively rare phenomenon would have to be corrected," which he seems to be moving toward embracing in the conclusion to that essay when he states: "Outside the realm of psychophysical parallelism . . . synchronicity is not a phenomenon whose regularity is at all easy to demonstrate."[12] This chapter will continue looking at aspects of mind-body resonance that may help address this point.

In particular, scientific attention has recently focused on refining correlations that have been made among a variety of discrete emotional states and specific, activated regions of the brain, especially as detected and mapped by functional magnetic resonance imaging (fMRI).[13] The relative ease and speed of "contagion" of emotions between individuals is well known, for example, Orson Welles's radio broadcast, as if it were an actual news event, of H. G. Wells's "The War of the Worlds" created widespread panic, with people telephoning their friends and relatives across the United States spreading the panic; more direct and immediate forms of emotional contagion can be seen in the behavior of crowds, as when in the grip of a demagogue. However, emotional contagion also has a positive side, most likely an adaptive aspect, as it can support social interactions and relations, and is thought to be one of the foundations of empathic resonance.[14]

Cognitive neuroscientists have measured the transmission of basic emotions such as anger, sadness, disgust, or joy as occurring within milliseconds, often without conscious awareness, though frequently with alterations in mood. Humans tend to spontaneously mimic and synchronize with the emotional behavior of others, especially those with whom they have some intimacy, often without consciously registering the phenomena. Reciprocally, evidence supports the role of imitation and mirroring of others as generating the psychosomatic conditions enhancing feelings of intimacy; hence, a strong correlation between the degree of imitative behavior and the capacity to empathize has been documented.[15] Similar research has shown that "mimicry increases prosocial behavior" and that "participants who had been mimicked were more helpful and generous toward other people than were nonmimicked participants."[16] Such observations have been put to use in many areas of modern life, from advertising products, to political campaigns, to criminal interrogation. The moral and ethical dimensions of the use of this research are left to those who employ it; some have called for public debate.[17] These studies have led to a view of the Self as inherently social and based in intersubjective experience.

Cues that may trigger a spread of emotions between people, such as facial expressions, body language, voice tone, speech rhythms, and so forth, associated with specific emotions, can also be studied for their capacity to activate various brain regions. Functional magnetic resonance imaging studies comparing the direct experience of an emotion with induced reactions to the same emotion (such as being shown images of faces clearly bearing the target emotion) display a number of striking similarities in the brain regions manifesting activity. Thus there is a neurophysiological base for the experience of resonance and transmission of emotions among people.

More broadly, comparative studies in zoology have revealed that the capacity for rapid, automatic emotional communications is a universal trait of the mammalian brain. Thus we humans seem to be evolutionarily adapted to transmit and receive emotional communications that in turn describe a fundamental affective dimension to empathy. Naturally there are myriad problems that can vex this system, inhibiting or impairing these capacities and resulting in clinical disorders such as autism and sociopathy.

Empathy, however, is not restricted to contagion or transmission of affects; it is far more complex. (For a recent summary of the neuroscientific data on empathy, including the multiple brain sites involved, see Jean Decety's "A Social Cognitive Neuroscience Model of Human Empathy.") Decety's framework considers empathy to involve

> parallel and distributed processing in a number of dissociable computational mechanisms. Shared neural representations, self-awareness, mental flexibility, and emotional regulation constitute the basic macro-components of empathy, which are mediated by specific neural systems [each of which are detailed in the article]. Consequently, damage to each of those components may lead to an alteration of empathic behavior and produce selective social disorders, depending on which aspect is disrupted.[18]

While a full discussion of this type of information is beyond the scope of this book, it is interesting to see how these contemporary scientific models lend some support to a model of the psyche as dissociable such as Jung postulated. The gap between a neurobiological formulation of the correlates of mind and the subjective experience of consciousness, including empathy of course, remains, so that the poetic manner in which the psyche meaningfully personifies its components, for example as figures or elements in dreams, continues to evoke mystery.

From developmental studies in addition to somatic and affective aspects of empathy, a further, slower system for processing and understanding the actions and appearance of others has been identified emerging from the mechanism of imitation. While infants are able to imitate certain behaviors (tongue protrusion) within hours of birth, the onset of the ability to engage in pretense and especially to recognize pretense in others normally develops between eighteen and twenty-four months. Preschoolers are known to be able to discern simple intentions of others, as Marco Iacoboni notes in describing research into this area: "the goal of the observed action is the primary factor in driving imitative behavior in preschoolers."[19] When asked by an adult researcher to "do as I do" these children will imitate as if in front of a mirror.[20] Our first experiences of symmetry are of mirroring, beginning with physical acts and gradually extending metaphorically to a way of knowing others' emotions and intentions. Empathy in its early forms relies heavily on mirroring, and in turn the impulse to symmetrize is a key element in our initial capacity to learn intersubjectively, even while we must go beyond this as the Self becomes more differentiated from others.

Somewhere between ages four to six years, normal children develop the ability to impute false beliefs to others, to cognitively recognize that others have minds like their own that have representations that can be true or false. Prior to this, children generally fail to comprehend the difference between what they know about a situation they have observed versus what others know about it. The classic form of the experiments on this were done by Heinz Wimmer and Josef Perner;[21] the setup is the use of an audio story or video clip in which a child places a desired object (toy, piece of chocolate, etc.) in one location, then leaves the room, followed by the appearance of an adult who moves the object to a second location. When asked where the child will look for the object when returning to the room, the majority of children under four years tend to point to the second location as if the child in the story has the same knowledge they have. However, even prior to this, children view others' actions as understandable from within their own viewpoint. This is not restricted to humans, or even primates or mammals, for example, "laboratory studies show that western scrub jays can know another bird's intentions and act on that knowledge. A jay that has stolen food itself, for example, knows that if another jay watches it hide a nut, there's a chance the nut will be stolen. So the first jay will return to move the nut when the other jay is gone."[22] Throughout childhood then, the "theory of mind" (TOM) by which children attempt to comprehend others gradually matures along with their brain and neural systems. In distinction to the affective component this more cognitively complex form of empathy takes place on a slower time scale; the brain regions involved differ significantly from those associated with the emotional processes.[23]

Developmental evidence does suggest that a preponderance of positive early attachment experiences facilitates maturation of empathy and TOM, while negative experiences of abuse or neglect inhibit this. Reparation of damage due to failures of empathy, past and present, both cognitive and affective, has become an important feature of many contemporary psychotherapies. The pathways of interaction between the two forms of empathy, however, have not yet been fully delineated, though they obviously are interconnected. While not forming a definitive bridge between different empathic processes, in the last decade there has been a fascinating set of related findings linking perception and action. These discoveries began in a research team headed by Giacomo Rizzolatti of the University of Parma, with a series of papers on a group of visio-motor neurons that are now termed *mirror neurons*. First observed in macaque monkeys, these neurons "discharge when the monkey *observes* an action made by another individual and [also] when it *executes* the same or similar action;"[24] however, these neurons will not fire when an action is pantomimed,[25] though they will fire when the animal anticipates that the action will occur, as when the object being grasped is hidden. The stimulus need not be visual, even the sound of the action in the dark can trigger the firing, the firing seems linked to the goal of the action. Evidence for human homologues of these neurons was soon reported in several brain sites, such as Broca's area, with its involvement in speech, as well as in other premotor cortices.[26]

Further studies have extended the finding on neurological mirroring to tactile, auditory, and pain stimulus in humans. For example, observing someone you are close to being pricked with a pin causes analogous pain circuitry to resonate in you, though usually with less intensity. This is likely due to the fact that it is the affective more than the sensory elements of the pain network that are activated by the mirror neurons as demonstrated in these studies.[27] In addition, these neurons also offer an important, primitive (foundational) component of the neurological substrate for aspects of "the capacity to represent mental states of others by means of a conceptual system, commonly designated as 'Theory of Mind.'"[28]

There is growing evidence that mirroring processes are involved across a spectrum of emotional resonances, feeling responses, and cognitive reflections on others' actions, as well as being a fundamental part of the origins and development of language. An excellent review of the major areas of research into mirror neurons can be found in a new book by Iacoboni.[29] In this he delineates a hierarchy of mirror neurons with varying tasks: strictly congruent mirror neurons that "fire for identical actions, either performed or observed;[30] broadly congruent mirror neurons that "fire at the sight of an action that is not necessarily identical to the executed action but achieves a similar goal;[31] logically related mirror neurons that are implicated in "coding not simply the observed action but also the intention associated with it;[32] super mirror neurons that "may be conceptualized as a functional neuronal layer 'on top of' the classical mirror neurons, controlling and modulating their activity";[33] and Iacoboni suggests they "may represent a wonderfully simple neural distinction between self and other."[34] Iacoboni sees mirror neurons as being formed and shaped by social interactions, starting with the mother-infant dyad, and being essential to self-recognition.[35] Further, he states: "Clearly, mirror neurons learn to predict the actions of other people. This ability was not present at birth . . . the mirror neuron system may be shaped by experience."[36]

Culture and biology are finding a meeting point in these systems; they form one of the links between psyche and soma, and may be a means of exploring the psychoid realm. However, the mechanisms of neural plasticity and neurogenesis applied to mirror neurons have not yet been delineated.

The discovery of mirror neurons has generated intense multidisciplinary interest in intersubjective forms of communication, beginning with imitation and mimicry and progressing to simulating the mind of others as a way of grasping their intentions. Unfortunately, perhaps unavoidably, in the midst of all of this wonderful scientific research there has been limited attention to the deeper subjective meanings associated with the measurements. Perhaps a fruitful collaboration between neuroscientists and analysts will emerge, as a number of the scientists are aware of analytic theories in general and do see some correlations.

A significant attempt to link the mirror neuronal research with philosophical ideas has been through simulation theory (ST), which is an empathy theory, investigating mental imitation. Through attenuated mimicry of the body state of another, which may involve only microscopic muscular changes as in facial expressions, often outside conscious awareness, relevant activations of matching brain regions in the observer permit a form of social knowledge to be communicated, for example, feeling a sense of heightened danger then realizing someone nearby is in an agitated, angry state. Couched in the language of "mind-reading," ST is based on the premise that people use their own minds to mimic the minds of others, discerning goals and intentions without the need to replicate overt behaviors—clinical, therapeutic empathy draws heavily on just such resonance capacities. Activated complexes can suppress, distort, or intensify what is "read" by one person from the action of another; hence, we can detect psychopathological features associated with such misreadings, including some forms of transference. The psychological theories of William James, whom Jung admired, and Rudolph Hermann Lotze, a nineteenth-century philosopher whom Jung refers to on several occasions,[37] form an important historical backdrop to the ideomotor model[38] implicit in ST. I also believe there is a natural link between Jung's model of the psyche and human interactions and these current theories of empathy. Analogously some schools of acting employ these kinds of simulation mechanisms both to build characters and to communicate them to audiences;[39] the methods they use can be adapted to the Jungian practice of active imagination leading to new insights as we embody personifications from our inner imagery, trying them on to learn from them empathically.

Role-playing and more generally the capacity to take part in interactive play are seen in ST as a key element in the maturation of imitative learning. Alvin Goldman, a philosopher and chief exponent of ST—he has written a major text in this area[40]—notes that it has been "found that children who engaged in more joint play, including role play, performed better on mind-reading tasks, but no such connection was found for solitary pretense."[41] Extrapolated to psychotherapeutic training, ST could have profound consequences. For example, the nondefensive exploration in supervision of transference/countertransference enactments with their conscious and unconscious role-play scenarios[42] could provide a means to enhance the empathic attunement of therapists to patients as well as between therapists and supervisors.

Yet deficits in or dysfunctions of mirror neuron systems may produce some limitations to empathic capabilities. In one of the more extreme examples, malfunctioning of mirror neuron systems has been proposed as contributing to the basic problems involved in autism with the known failures to imitate or to coordinate self-other representations. Iacoboni discusses both the research findings and the therapeutic strategies that are emerging based on the new understanding of autism in terms of mirror neurons.[43] More speculatively, the attachment hunger of certain types of patients who have suffered basic attachment injuries may be predicated on inadequate activation of incipient mirror neuronal systems during early development. The core dilemmas resulting from failures in primary object relations that leave some individuals perpetually scanning others for microshifts in affective expression, as has been discussed in the Jungian literature for "borderline patients,"[44] would be one area for further investigation.

Moral and ethical concerns are also raised by the study of mirror neurons and imitative capacities. Philosopher Jesse Prinz has articulated moral milestones beginning with newborns' attempts at facial mimicry and very young children's susceptibility to emotional contagion, underscoring the key foundational role of imitative capacities in moral development; this leads him to claim that "a bad imitator is likely to form unstable attachments."[45] Applying this to the study of psychopaths, Prinz notes that they "can imitate the behaviors of others to a reasonable degree, but they cannot imitate the emotional states of others, and this has serious implications for competence and conduct."[46] Thus the affective recognition and response to what is seen as evil may well emerge from a core capacity to access imitative processes, and moral maturation may hinge on our creative use of those processes. Additional, related topics that the study of mirror neurons has offered to shed light on, so far, are imitative violence linked to the media[47] and addictive behaviors—social cues tied to addictive behaviors often play a role in relapses.[48]

Empathy should not be confused with sympathy; it can be used in noncompassionate ways. At the extreme, consider the torturer who seeks to intensify the experience of pain, physical and mental, by understanding the weakness and vulnerabilities of the one being tortured. Such an individual would need to be able to empathically locate pain and fear in the mental states of his victim to maximize effectiveness. The capacity for empathic attunement is thus morally neutral, and to be therapeutic ethical discernment is required.

As noted, in terms of symmetry in psychological systems, empathy permits a temporary symmetrizing, linking Self and Other (person or object) in a unifying field. For therapeutically useful psychological reflection to emerge from this state of immersion a breaking of the transitory symmetrization will need to occur eventually. This can then lead to the full emergence of empathic understanding. Empathy then is a connecting principle that links us to our world in ways that feel deeply meaningful, especially when we can step back and reflect on our experience (that is, upon breaking the symmetry). As we have seen, the causes that activate the empathic systems are often unconscious with a psychoid quality, that is, beyond our capacity for awareness and can feel as an acausal coincidence. Therefore, I suggest that there can be a synchronistic field dimension to our empathic experiences.

## The Analytic Field

To enhance the clinical utility of the ideas on empathy being presented here, I will return to a discussion of the analytic field. One of the most distinctive aspects of C. G. Jung's model of the psyche is his postulation of a core level, the collective unconscious, operating underneath the personal conscious and unconscious aspects of the mind. This deeper layer is comprised of the network of all archetypes, where archetypes are the formal patterns, without content, the universal propensities of psychological life capable of expressing themselves across the spectrum of human experience from the instinctual to the sublime. When realized concretely, archetypes manifest through affect-laden images of a transpersonal nature, often with a numinous quality.

As discussed in chapter 3, there is a scale-free or fractal quality to the collective unconscious. By shifting focus from the global polycentric network of the collective to one specific archetype another parallel network at a reduced scale is encountered. This can be made evident by examining the network of associations and links that emerge through the process of amplification—applying cultural and historical analogies to symbolic material in order to bring archetypal aspects of the material into clearer view, often for therapeutic purposes. General and specific forms were presented in chapter 3 (see figs. 3 and 4 respectively)—the reduction of symmetry with attendant relaxing of rigidity and polarization of the models in moving from the first and second generation of Jungians is clear; by the third generation we are moving toward a scale-free network model for analytic methods like amplification.[49]

An ancient, profoundly philosophical network image with multiple levels of nested mirroring that was mentioned in chapter 2 is "Indra's net" (*Yin-t'o-lo kang*) from Indian and Chinese Buddhist philosophy; it is used in the Hua-yen school—the primary sūtra of this school, the Flower Garland Sūtra,[50] is regarded in the Mahūyūna tradition as the Buddha's first sermon. This sūtra emphasizes interdependence; it is a radical field model. Analogs from fractal geometry have been recognized recently by Western mathematicians.[51] The convergence of introverted Eastern meditative practices with extraverted Western science has produced resonant images of "objective truth"; an example is the image on the cover of this book, The Glowing Limit—"the glowing yellow lacework manifests entirely of its own accord out of the initial arrangement of just five touching red circles."[52]

While a full explication of the analogy of Indra's net with a Jungian model of the collective unconscious or an archetypal view of empathy is beyond the scope of this text, we can note that this mirroring "net" metaphorically offers the viewer a wholly interconnected universe, in which all of the parts are interdependent and mutually conditioned. These tenets also form the core of a holistic, emergentist viewpoint, which when applied to human relationships is the paradigm gaining ascendancy in the analytic world. As previously mentioned, Jung presaged this network model in various remarks about the interwovenness of the archetypes in the psyche, the deepest source of human patterns and hence, implicit, the source of all wisdom. The third patriarch of Hua-yen, Fa Tsang, explicating this net of interrelatedness saw it as especially true of the "unending relationships between wisdom and compassion."[53]

In the language of Jungian psychology, the energizing or activation of an archetypal node is frequently referred to as a particular pattern having "constellated," for example, the propensity to face adversity with determination to vanquish it may reflect the constellation of a heroic archetype in a person's life. However, such activations by their nature are transgressive of any view of a person as a wholly isolated entity; inner and outer environments are necessarily part of the full pattern, also in accord with the finding on mirror neurons. At deeper levels the psyche is not a closed system but opens into a field of interactions among individuals, a network with strong and weak links that can become self-organizing.

In Jung's great study, "The Psychology of the Transference,"[54] he presents an archetypal viewpoint with alchemical amplifications of this seemingly most personal of therapeutic problems. His exploration of the deep background to transference phenomena brings him to postulate a bipersonal interactive field model for the analytic relationship. Mario Jacoby[55] subsequently adapted this for more general use with the now well-known diagram (fig. 9) in which we have a four-node interaction among the patient (P), the analyst (A), and the unconscious of each, generating a field in which the analytic process is occurring.

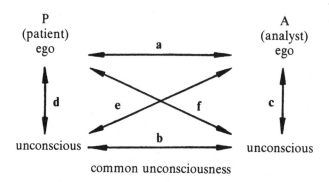

*Figure 9. Analyst-patient field. Reproduced from Mario Jacoby, (1984),*
The Analytic Encounter. *Toronto: Inner City Books, p. 25.*

While it would be instructive to explore in detail the vicissitudes of empathy along each of the pathways shown, my focus will be restricted to a process starting with "emotional contagion." The unconscious, affectively resonant aspect of empathy would operate along path "b" in figure 9 and can impact psyche and soma. Jung refers to this variously as *participation mystique* as a general psychological issue, and "psychic" or "unconscious infection" when an illness is transferred from patient to analyst. The dyad is then said to be in a state of "mutual unconsciousness," through a mechanism analogous to the Kleinian notion of projective identification.[56] To the open and receptive, or "empty" mind, this can induce an activating resonance.

Turning to a clinical example: a man in his early thirties with obsessional difficulties had been in treatment with me for about a year when we had the following session. We met at the last hour of a rather long day, not his usual time; I had accepted a request from him to reschedule several weeks prior due to a time conflict. The session turned out to be laborious for me. While I was familiar with the constricted states that often accompanied his difficulties in expressing himself, especially when feelings were involved, I felt unusually trapped and exhausted as the hour wore on. In the closing minutes of the session, the patient surprisingly produced a dream that contained the image of figure in a closet. There was no time for associations or exploration of the imagery. After he left, I felt so depleted that I needed to lie down and rest before driving home. I felt on the verge of the flu; however, curiously I felt fine the next day. The discrepancy signaled that path "b" might be active.

Working through such dilemmas begins with an act of recognition; the analyst's consciously identifying the affect or somatic state activated as associated with the ingested "projection"—opening the mind. Next, cognitive empathy by the analyst for his/her own distressed internal state employs reflective understanding of the history and meaning of such activations within the analyst's own psychology. This initiates internal empathic repair of the ego-Self axis, path "c" in figure 9.

Returning to the case, the following week we met at our usual daytime hour. Not surprisingly, the overt affective aspect of the field was not much altered from the week before. The patient did not seem to have noticed my state of fatigue or distress in the previous session—no references or derivatives were detectable in the subsequent material raised and discussed, that is, no direct evidence of activity along path "f." However, through my attention to and empathic resonance with the figure in the closet (path "e"), which I now experienced more directly in terms of the trapped, silenced, and frustrated feelings I had been accepting previously without adequate reflection, we were able to explore the images of the dream left at the door. This also points to an important aspect of the use of empathy in analytic work involving unconscious material: an empathic field can be active with figures outside the conscious personality, the ego. In ordinary relationships awareness of empathy is often restricted to the conscious personality of the other. Working with dreams opens up a much broader range of empathic possibilities, and awareness of the impact of unconscious processes can often be transmitted through empathic understanding of non-ego figures in dreams. This can be a shock for the ego, which may be troped toward such personifications through skillful direction from the analyst.

Once the analyst has been able to restore an internal empathic awareness, the task becomes one of communication with the patient. This can flow along conscious (path "a") and/or unconscious (path "e") channels with resulting empathic understanding or repair both between the partners of the dyad and in the internal world of the patient, (re-)establishing at least transitory ego-Self connection in the patient (path "d").

In the case at hand, the shift in my attitude facilitated by acknowledging to myself of my previous discomforts together with a growing awareness of care and concern for elements of the psyche that had been repressed, caused me to speak with the patient about how I'd felt a mix of constraint and concern at the end of the last hour. I wondered aloud as to whether this had any relevance to the figure in the dream. In response he identified the figure as a child and began to tentatively associate to the child. As he seemed in danger of depleting his associations and falling back into a more constricted state, I attempted to facilitate a more freely associative process by asking the age of the child in the closet. This resulted in his revealing a piece of his history previously undisclosed. His associations to that time in his life included mention of a specific illness, the symptoms of which were remarkably similar to what I had experienced after the session the previous week—and I had had a serious childhood illness with an onset at roughly the same age, though not of the same type. With the emergence of this link I could more fully grasp the importance of path "b" for communications with this patient. During the next phase of the analysis, the child of the dream came to be understood by us as representing a time in his life when much of his natural spontaneity had receded. By beginning to get the frightened, frozen playfulness "out of the closet" a starting point was found for some long, at times torturous work on obsessional defenses that had been locked in at a somatic level. The key recognition for me in this encounter had been of the synchronistic aspect in the psychosomatic field (the transitory but meaningful illness), an "objective intuition" that only became useful when brought to consciousness.

## Conclusion

Within the context of the diagram (fig 9) I offer the conjecture that mirror neurons operate as field resonators, contributing to the neural apparatus that allows detection of the vicissitudes of the intersubjective, analytic "third" through empathic channels. The "third" could be understood as emerging from the combined pathways of fig 9, especially those in the central region (paths a, b, e, and f). In the present case registering the emergence of the mercurial child as the "third" (co-constructed from our mutual experiences, conscious and unconscious, atop an archetypal base) was crucial to the fate of the analytic process. I believe the emergence of the third in the field was facilitated by the unconscious affective attunement or mirroring that when processed with conscious empathy supported the intensifying constellation and subsequent use of the "wounded-healer" pattern in the field—this third is a property of the field not simply in/of the analyst, in this case myself. Thus empathy when combined with the processing of countertransference reactions is not constrained solely to be an introspective examination through brief "trial" identification of the mental worlds of the other but actually a way of experiencing the resonant field itself, like the emerging pattern in the "Glowing Limit"; and more generally a way of engaging in and with the world, especially that of the analysand.

The argument follows that while mirror neurons can aid empathic communication generally, they may be of special help to those who adopt a Jungian approach in detecting archetypal patterns as they begin to constellate in the therapeutic process. Their roles, however lowly or primitive (or more sophisticated, as with "super mirror neurons"), are essential in facilitating links between conscious and unconscious experience. Thus they foster an aspect of the instantiation of the transcendent function, contributing to making it an embodied, psychosomatic reality, which in turn can continue to mature throughout life, especially as they themselves are shaped by experience. Similarly, since empathy is known to be essential in valuing the other, a key aspect of an ethical attitude, the study and cultivation of all of its components at manifold levels of abstraction should be of paramount importance both during and after training of the therapist.

Science has not yet identified the embryological origins of the mirroring system, or how much of the mirror neuronal systems are present at birth, though it is now clear that much of its capacities emerge through social learning and interaction. The degree to which this system has plasticity and is capable of modification makes its study of great interest to anyone interested in psychotherapeutic training. Likewise, the gap from the behavior of mirror neurons to our lived empathic experience remains mysterious. Perhaps this is where Lipps's original views about empathy being both internal imitation and a special form of knowledge are most relevant. In the language of this book we might say that empathic knowing involves both a holistic impression as well as an intuition of what is emergent in our experience of an other.

More broadly, the well-known neuroscientist V. S. Ramachandran (of phantom limb fame) claims the discovery of mirror neurons with relevance to human evolution "is the single most important 'unreported' story of the decade."[57] He discusses the evolutionary importance of mirror neurons and their role in the transmission of culture in his recent book *A Brief Tour of Human Consciousness*.[58] There is also a possible connection to R. Dawkins's meme theory that could be considered. This would provide a bridge between neurological and cultural learning.[59] Our evolved capacity for empathic understanding of ourselves and our world is what makes us most fully human. Some contemporary philosophers feel that empathy is the precondition for consciousness. Viewed as an emergent aspect of brain-mind I suggest there is an underlying synchronistic core to empathic experience that can be described in terms of a resonant field. Perhaps an additional step toward the resonance among different cultural appreciations of mind can be taken now; my hope is that we are coming upon a crossroads where much more dialogue will be possible.

## CHAPTER 5

# Cultural Synchronicities

In the previous chapter we looked at a particular type of emergent phenomenon in dyadic relationships. The broad suggestion was that there is a synchronistic dimension to empathy. While acknowledging some of the neurophysiologic underpinnings of empathy, we also treated it as a field phenomenon. Discrete moments of intensified empathic attunement are postulated to have emergent qualities that share features with the description of synchronicity that has been put forward in this book. At this point we will shift our attention toward larger systems of a sociopolitical nature or representatives of a cultural Zeitgeist of a particular age, that is, to collective phenomena. In particular, events that can be identified as having intensely emergent and synchronistic features about them will be the focus, what I will speak of as "cultural synchronicities."

## The Emergence of Democracy

In a recent publication I discussed the origins of democracy in fifth-century (BCE) Athens.[1] These origins are of particular interest for our topic, specifically the findings of scholars who have noted new conceptions of time as it is understood, experienced, and represented, that is, changing views of temporality linked with the new forms of political life emerging during this period. Thus Christian Meier's[2] notion of the emergence of "political time" for the Athenians who were moving toward democracy, has been expanded on by Csapo and Miller,[3] who explore the interactive relationship between temporality and power. Especially noteworthy in the shift from archaic/aristocratic to democratic political forms is the special attention they give to a term that may be recognizable to Jungian-oriented readers, *kairos*:

In the Archaic period, *kairos* was associated with a critical place or appropriate and just measure, but in the fifth century its meaning becomes predominantly temporal. . . . *Kairos* captures the act of decision in the intensity of the briefest possible moment; in some contexts the word means "criterion," "judgment," or the act of decision itself. A semantic fusion of ideas about time and ideas about knowledge . . . *kairos* permits one to triumph over contingency.[4]

Seizing the right moment politically (*kairos* as the "nick of time") was seen to manifest in the appearance of consensus within the assembly of the *demos* (the political body comprised of the voting citizens, itself an emergent entity); this consensus was also viewed as an expression of harmony within the group and when well-functioning was a source of tolerance, both important democratic principles. How then does the evolving idea of *kairos* link to our theme?

Richard Onians,[5] in his *The Origins of European Thought* (a useful source for amplificatory information), has a chapter on *kairos* in which he draws on etymology to identify two predominate metaphors from the archaic period in Greece. The first is hitting the mark in archery, the archer's use of the combination of true aim and strength to penetrate defenses such as armor; and second, weaving, passing the shuttle through the openings formed by the warp threads. As stated, with the onset of democratic forms of governance this notion becomes more time oriented; the desired opening becomes the unique, opportune moment rather than just the right spot. More broadly, space and time also take on a more interactive mode in the democratic world, implicitly drawing on what has been identified here as field models.

It is in the dynamic, temporal sense that Jung generally employs the term: "We are living in what the Greeks called the *kairos*—the right moment—for a 'metamorphosis of the gods,' of the fundamental principles and symbols. This peculiarity of our time, which is certainly not of our conscious choosing, is the expression of the unconscious man within us who is changing."[6] And, Marie-Louise von Franz in *Number and Time* brings this thinking directly into reflections on synchronicity: "in China number serves to determine the quality of synchronistic *kairoi* more accurately";[7] and later, "The association of *kairos* with goddesses weaving time alludes . . . to the idea of a 'field' in which 'meaningful connections,' are interwoven like threads of a fabric."[8]

In general the emergence of consensus in the democratic processes of an organization tends to reflect self-organizing aspects of the larger field formed by the individuals who comprise the voting body. The moment of consensus in this sense is an act of creation of the whole that has a synchronistic falling together in time at its core and hence evidence of an emerging archetypal constellation. The feeling of rightness of what comes forth in such moments can often be detected by some sense of the numinous, or of a "third" that all partake in. Naturally this needs to be followed up by conscious reflection and discernment for comprehension of the meaning and course of action to be determined from such consensus, or the *demos* can fall apart into a mob.

Within this context the notion of the *demos* itself deserves a bit more explication. Onians suggests that it derives from

the word for fat, a fat part of an animal, applied specifically to land. Homer seems to have thought so. . . . He uses δημος [*demos*] of the land occupied by a community—which would be the fertile land well covered with soil as opposed to the bare and barren rocks. . . . On each such δημος a community would develop and be referred to as a δημος just as we use "parish," "country," etc., for the inhabitants of the same.[9]

Here place is primary, as a deep sense of connection to a spot on the earth whose richness and bounty supports the community that lives and prospers off the "fat of the land." The term *demos* gradually became more metaphoric, the attachment was to the sense of belonging to the community. Identity shifts from physical location to the community living in that location, to more generally the communal body. Time is not explicit in the early formulations of the *demos*, but the shift noted does share with that of *kairos* in an increasingly dynamic quality.

While the pathway from communal identity to Athenian democracy had many elements, a crucial step came at the end of the sixth century BCE. For the following account I draw upon Manville and Ober.[10] In the face of the loss of the democratic process[11] with the invasion of the Spartans in 508 BCE, Cleisthenes used his visionary leadership in the surprising Athenian victory over the Spartans to institute a series of reforms. For the purposes of this text, the relevant aspect was Cleisthenes' revision of the *deme,* the system of membership in a local neighborhood (by this period every male Athenian over the age of eighteen was eligible to become a citizen by being formally voted into the local *deme*).

Now Cleisthenes redrew the *demes,* redistributing by lottery the entire population into ten new "tribes." These new *deme* were deliberately made up of individuals drawn from each of the major areas of the activity of the city (geographic and economic), especially farmers (agrarian villages), seafarers (coastal regions), and merchants (urban center). These ten composite units were then organized in such a fashion as to form the military and civic services, and their representatives formed the overall general assembly. Because of the large size of the assembly (the general body was a council of five hundred) and the short terms of office for most posts, most citizens had multiple opportunities over a lifetime to be directly involved in the political life of the city, to the point that "politics became the dominant element in the life of the community."[12]

The rearrangement and engagement of individuals into a network of networks to create complex wholes that have the capacity for self-organization strongly indicates this society was built on an intuition of what has been mentioned throughout this text as scale-free networks. Recall that one of their key features is emergent properties: individual interactions that combine, especially within a competitive environment, to form a linked network that has new features unforeseeable from the perspective of the interactions alone. The properties of the whole transcend any and all of the individuals and their interactions. These types of networks are highly robust to a variety of attacks, although knocking out major centers, "hubs," can cripple them.[13] Strikingly adaptive, they exhibit many features that suggest enhanced capacity for creative responses to their environments—and the Athenians were legendary for their remarkable endurance and innovative capacities in the face of adversity.

Thus Cleisthenes deserves to be seen as the genius who first tapped into and orchestrated a fully emergent political process in a moment marked by *kairos,* which we have come to know as democracy. Not that all democracies have such vitality, or that once present they will simply persist; even the Athenian democracy flowered and then was overcome by external forces. Similarly, emergent systems are not without shadows, in fact, they often are morally and ethically ambiguous, requiring thoughtful reflection to remain grounded in such values. Further, emergence is not a static condition but can be readily lost to inflexible forms; it requires ongoing efforts to stay near the edge of order and chaos if it is to remain a viable option.

Extending this to contemporary organizational life, what processes might we envision being of assistance in building vibrant democratic forms? While an in-depth analysis cannot be embarked on here, one area can be noted: in seeking to build a pluralistic, participatory culture, conflict resolution often plays a key role. How difficult matters and tensions between groups or individuals are handled can make tremendous difference for an organization; building consensus that holds rather than collapses diversity can lead to unanticipated creative solutions. One important means for holding such tensions is mediation services. In passing I would note that mediation processes tend to have a dialectic aspect where the tensions between differing positions (minority versus majority views) need to be held in such a manner as to facilitate the appearance of an emergent (and asymmetric) third. As discussed in various of my previous publications,[14] the appearance of such a third tends to be heralded by a synchronistic event. Thus I return to my main point: recognition of the role of synchronistic phenomena in providing unique opportunities for emergent processes to appear in focused group activities. This is an area that deserves much further study as it has great implications for many aspects of our collective life. In turning to our second example, however, a cautionary note will be sounded, not all emergent process foster diversity, at times just the opposite can occur.

# The "Conquest" of Mexico (a very brief history)

In late 1518 the Spanish governor of Cuba commissioned Hernán Cortés to lead an expedition to the mainland of Mexico solely for the purpose of establishing trade. An opportunist Cortés leaped to this chance and in fact sailed on 18 February 1519 in great haste to escape a potential revocation of his commission. After exploits in the Yucatán, including gaining interpreters, Cortés made his way to what is today Veracruz. He arrived on Good Friday, 22 April 1519. With a relatively small force (he had eleven ships with about one hundred sailors and 530 soldiers), he quickly established alliances with communities that were in tension with the Aztecs, the lords of mainland Central Mexico. Before the end of the year, after a variety of battles and confrontations, Cortés and his men made their way to Tenochtitlán, the Aztec capital (at the site of today's Mexico City) where they were ambivalently welcomed by the ruler Moctezuma II.

The Spaniards rapidly established dominance despite their inferior position militarily, even with their armor, horses, and firearms. They maintained their fragile control over the city until the people rose up against them in July 1520. Driven into retreat, the Spanish were gradually able to regroup, reestablish alliances with other indigenous groups, and return to the offensive. They eventually laid siege successfully to Tenochtitlán, which surrendered to them on 13 August 1521. While the conquest of Mesoamerica continued over the next sixty years, the remarkable success of Cortés has some extraordinary features when evidence reportedly from the Aztec side is considered. The impact of these events on the shaping of the modern world has been enormous.

While there are certainly many factors involved in Cortés's success, including his own craftiness and strategic abilities, a group of scholars of Mesoamerican history have helped create a picture of some of the cultural and psychological factors influencing the Aztecs in their ambivalent dealings with the Spaniards. Most prominent in these narratives is the place of the myth/legend of Quetzalcoatl. Aztec sovereignty rested upon a legitimacy deriving from their Toltec ancestry through a link to Quetzalcoatl.

In Aztec culture there was a strong belief in the eventual return of a royal ancestor who would "shake the foundation of heaven" and who would conquer the city of Tenochtitlán, as told by David Carrasco, a historian of religions at Princeton in his *Quetzalcoatl and the Irony of Empire*.[15] In the distant past there had been a Toltec priest-king, Topiltzin Quetzalcoatl—sharing the name and becoming conflated with the wind god Ehécatl Quetzalcoatl, the plumed serpent—who was said to have reigned during a near golden age. Tricked, deceived, and shamed by a sorcerer into fleeing his native Tollan, Topiltzin Quetzalcoatl disappeared into the east, either by immolation with subsequent ascension into the heavens to become the morning star (our Venus), or sailing away on a raft constructed of snakes.[16] Additionally, Quetzalcoatl was said to have made a set of arrows on his disappearance and according to the millenarian beliefs of the Aztecs, the astrological type of year in which he returns would determine who would be struck down by him with his arrows.[17]

The year 1519 in the Aztec calendar not only coincided with birth and death dates of Topiltzin Quetzalcoatl, but if he were to reappear in the year "1 Reed" (which 1519 was) he was prophesized to strike down kings.[18] Even more unusual are a set of portrayals of Quetzalcoatl (the Mayan Kukulkan) as a bearded, light-skinned warrior—see UCLA anthropologist H. B. Nicholson's *Topiltzin Quetzalcoatl: The Once and Future Lord of the Toltecs*,[19] especially in a culture where facial hair was rare.[20] There are further striking coincidences in this story, including a series of ten omens observed in the years before the Spanish arrived. The cumulative effect was to create consternation, confusion, and doubt in the Aztecs, but especially in Moctezuma's mind. According to reports gathered from native witnesses, the apparent return of Quetzalcoatl left Moctezuma "terror struck . . . he was filled with great dread, swooning. His soul was sickened, his heart was anguished."[21] It is reported that he remarked: "What will now befall us? . . . In great torment is my heart, as if it was washed in chili water."[22] Carrasco recognizes this: "His chili-water heart has taken on the character of what Rudolph Otto calls a 'creature feeling' of numinous dread, awe, and urgency. . . . He is encountering his numen, the origin of rulership, and it is an uncanny experience."[23] The throne was seen to belong to the ancestors; by his return Quetzalcoatl not only reclaims political authority but also asserts cosmological order.

In this mythic drama, clearly an archetype has constellated and synchronistic events are at play. However, this is not an experience of regeneration; instead, it fits a pattern of chaos and dissolution, a catastrophic end of an age. This was actually an aspect of Aztec myth, there had been four previous eras, all ending in disasters. The events could therefore be seen as an archetypal enactment at play on the stage of history.

A similar enactment a decade later allowed Cortés's second cousin, the conquistador Francisco Pizarro, access into Peru that would lead to a victory against enormous military odds over the Incas. As Carrasco reports: "According to several historical accounts, the Inca ruler [Atahuallpa] meets Pizarro and believes that 'it was Viracocha (the god) who had come just as he had promised them when he went away . . . And he gave thanks to Virachocha because he was coming at the appointed time.'"[24]

At the personal level we see repeated opportunism with a willingness to use the extraordinary coincidences associated with the archetypal pattern of return, but here in the service of greed and domination. The catastrophic results for the indigenous populations of the misattribution of the meaning of the emerging events should serve as a clear warning to any general idealization of synchronicities as evidence of utopian spirituality.

As Jung often cautioned when dealing with activated unconscious material, reflection on the attitude of consciousness toward such material as well as the need to carefully examine the moral implications arising from it are essential to psychological maturation. Robert Aziz,[25] in his first book on synchronicity, develops Jung's point, identifying various types of pathological reactions to synchronistic events when there is a lack of differentiation between self and the experience. Recognizing the tendencies to misuse coincidence to enhance a feeling of power or narcissistic grandiosity provides insight to these narratives. The usurpation of synchronicities can operate at collective as well as personal levels. Thus, many of the attempts in the sixteenth and seventeenth centuries by European commentators to gather detailed information on the events of the conquest, especially from the perspective of the indigenous peoples, were met with suppression.

Reflections on the significance of these events elaborating the psychological impact of the manner in which they have been used to foster Eurocentric colonial agendas has only begun to emerge in the aftermath of World War II in the era of postcolonial studies. Jung himself lived at the end of the colonial period; his comments about his travels reveal his colonial attitudes about the psychology/mind of "primitives" versus "Europeans," however, in fairness to him, much of the literature giving new perspective on these events has only developed after his death. Nevertheless, the synchronicity thesis was published less than a decade after the end of World War II as the great sociopolitical upheavals leading toward the postcolonial world were emerging. When the transgressive nature of synchronicity is accented we more readily acknowledge its contribution to the erosion of the classical boundaries of subject and object, with inner and outer worlds fully interpenetrating and becoming amalgamated in the psychoid archetype. This view moves us toward postcolonial discourse. Living on the cusp of great changes Jung frequently demonstrates this mixture of entrenchment in old attitudes while periodically breaking out of these in brilliant insights. I suggest his synchronicity concept, aligned with the radical aspect of the new physics as he understood it, was indeed seeking such a leap into the new and was a part of the postcolonial Zeitgeist. How then might a view informed by synchronicity reimagine the coincidences of the conquest narratives?

Beginning with the acknowledgment of mutuality of influence, even if asymmetric, is essential. A clash of cultures and religions in any meeting, as between sixteenth-century Europeans and the peoples of the Americas, was likely to have been inevitable, but the use of mythic coincidences solely for purposes of subjugation and theft also meant the unempathic, complete disregard of an opportunity for reflection and an inability to learn from the other except in an exploitive manner.

In one of the omens prior to the arrival of the Spaniards, Moctezuma saw "a strange creature . . . a bird the color of ashes . . . which wore a strange mirror in the crown of its head" and in this he further saw "people moving across a distant plain, spread out in ranks and coming forward in great haste"; this was a smoky mirror associated with the sorcerer—Tezcatlipoca whose name means smoky mirror—who originally tricked Quetzalcoatl. In one version Tezcatlipoca presented Quetzalcoatl with a mirror wrapped in cotton; Quetzalcoatl had never known that he had a human face and when this was revealed he fled in terror, abandoning the Aztecs to Huitzilopochtli, the one who demands human sacrifice.[26] Carrasco notes this vision is very similar to "Quetzalcoatl in Tollan, it is a mirror which reflects a great crisis in the land."[27] The need to learn about the other through reflection, though guided by fear and self-interest, is operating here, however concretely. For Cortés reflection comes from his armor; it is as if he embodies the smoky mirroring, letting others see what they want or fear in/through him.

In an article on Toltec mirrors, Renee Bergland begins by quoting a translation of an Aztec poem by Denise Levertov:

> *The true artist: capable, practicing, skillful;*
> *Maintains dialogue with his heart, meets things with his*
> *mind.*[28]

Bergland takes this as an apt description of what is needed for cross-cultural dialogue. But given Moctezuma's culture of human sacrifice, cutting out the hearts of others, meeting the heartless cruelty of Cortés's ambition, the possibility for a dialogic encounter and a meeting of minds is foreclosed upon from the onset. The synchronistic opportunity then is reduced to a kind of pseudo-empathic manipulation and a means of gaining power over the other. It is as if in Tezcatlipoca fashion, Cortez sets off another abandonment of the indigenous peoples to Huitzilopochtli in the conquest and its aftermath. Thus it seems to have taken 450+ years or more to begin to have some tools with which to reconsider the coincidence of such encounters, to reflect some heart back into them. Neither a prophetic reading nor identification with the source of synchronistic experience will work. Recognizing the mutuality, however asymmetric, of a moment of synchronicity is the first step in seeing the field one is in. When this is refused then the (archetypal) enactment is passed on; one cannot become identified with a god without great risk of sharing the fate of that god. This is a likely course for abused synchronicities, they become enactments that have a fated repetition about them. Perhaps we are reaching the place culturally that we can begin to metabolize these enactments and so more fully appreciate the significance of the original synchronicities.

In passing it should be noted that the image/metaphor of the mirror returns as a leitmotif in these pages. Recall Pauli's mirror complex that came to the fore when he could not accept the breaking of parity/symmetry in the events associated with weak nuclear forces. Or, how Jung's diagram of the layers of the psyche in his private letter to Victor White was restricted to mirror symmetry, much lower than the rigid symmetry of the figure published in *Aion*. Then, there are the mirror neurons that seem to form the physiological basis of the capacity for empathy. Now we arrive at cultural mirrors and the difficulties of discerning the "other" across gaps that seem initially unbridgeable. What one ends up seeing in these situations seems to be more an uncertain reflection of one's own unconscious concerns than a true picture of the other. I believe one function of synchronicities is to alert us to these gaps, to challenge us to see the emergent rather than magical wishes or fears.

In passing, a similar example can be found in the story of Captain James Cook's eighteenth-century encounter with the Hawaiians, where he was mistaken for the god Lono. This time, however, there were several sets of synchronicities, and the results were quite different for the European. Cook's arrival in Hawaii in early 1779 apparently coincided with rituals that were associated with the return of the year god Lono, a time of peace.[29] Cook subsequently left the Hawaiian Islands safely but due to the need for ship repairs he returned about a month later. However, the ritual season had shifted and it was now the time of Kū, the god of war, and Cook may have been less than welcome. Strife with the Hawaiians broke out and Cook was killed in the skirmish. Insensitivity to shifts in mythic patterns resulted in tragic coincidences, again suggesting caution in reading emergent patterns.

# The Discovery of Phosphorus

Let's return once again to the seventeenth century as the transition toward the modern world with the development of the scientific method was underway—a time when alchemy had its final flourish and chemistry was born. In this mix, in about 1669 an alchemist from Hamburg, Hennig Brandt, in search of the philosopher's stone, accidentally produced an extraordinary material that spontaneously burned in the air with a pale green glow, luminescent even when kept in a stoppered vessel. This material had been isolated from boiling down quantities of human urine. Brandt had unknowingly discovered the thirteenth element of what would later become the periodic table, phosphorus. The name comes from the Greek φωσ–φορος: light bringing, which in Latin is "Lucifer," the morning star—Cortes's deliberate misuse of Quetzalcoatl identity shares this archetypal quality—the morning star. The ironic aptness of the name *phosphorus* was gradually to be revealed.[30]

A pompous man, Brandt was prone to bragging about this new material but was caught in the dilemma of trying to simultaneously keep secret the method of its preparation. Brandt finally openly revealed the existence of the material in 1675, but by this time others had learned to take advantage of it, surmising how he must have obtained it. In fact, the only reason we know of Brandt as the discoverer is because one of the alchemists who was able to exploit the discovery commercially, Daniel Kraft, had been in Hanover demonstrating it for profit to the Duke Johann Frederick of Saxony whose historian and librarian, G. W. Leibniz, was in the audience. A few months later Leibniz was in Hamburg and by chance met Brandt. After learning the story Leibniz was able to secure Brandt employment with the duke as a resident alchemist. Leibniz went on to help Brandt make the material and published the way to produce it; we know of Brandt's role through Leibniz's papers.[31]

The story has additional acts as Kraft went in 1677 to England, where on the fifteenth of September he gave a demonstration to Robert Boyle, one of the founders of the science of chemistry, together with some of his friends. Boyle already knew of the discovery, as

Leibniz had written to Robert Hooke, the secretary of the Royal Society, prior to this. Boyle went on to study the properties of phosphorus in what are regarded as the very first experiments in chemistry. Thus phosphorus is the pivotal element in the changing approach to the world, which has come to be known as science at the very time it was emerging. Boyle and many others of the time felt that because of its extraordinary properties phosphorus must have healing properties. Because its luminescence was best seen at night, Boyle dubbed it *aerial nocticula,* spirit of the night light.[32]

Moving into the eighteenth century and the Age of Enlightenment, phosphorus was mistakenly imagined to have miraculous healing powers—in fact in its elemental form it's a dangerous poison, though oxidized as phosphates it is harmless. Because of its properties, it was imagined to be an aphrodisiac, called the *flammula vitae,* the vital flame of life. Some people even applied ointments embedded with it to their genitals in an attempt at "venereal excitation" (serious skin irritations, burns, and wounds could result) so that warnings against this had to be issued. Clearly the physical attributes were catching unconscious projections of forbidden, (demonic) erotic fantasies around the source of fire glowing in the night.

More broadly, the appearance of this element captures something of the Zeitgeist of the Age of Enlightenment with its glorification of human reason as the new light by which everything could be understood. The Luciferian, shadow aspect of this perspective gradually emerged and eventually made way for the compensatory discovery of the unconscious, which included the *lumen naturae* (light of nature, in the dark), as Jung understood it from alchemy as an expression of the "Self" (see "On the Nature of the Psyche," paragraphs 388–96). As such this could be used as easily for destructive as for creative purposes. Phosphorus was to reveal its dark side over time.

In addition to the medical misuse of phosphorus, it was used commercially in matches, especially the "lucifer match." These matches, while providing an instant source of fire, were not "safety matches" and easily ignited. Fires with tragic deaths resulted from these matches until safety matches were developed. Furthermore, match factories employed children as young as six years old, often working twelve-hour days. In 1845 Hans Christian Andersen published "The Little Match Girl," in which a poor girls selling matches dies of cold on New Year's Eve after exhausting her supply of matches. By 1864 such abuses brought legislation setting minimum age and number of hours of work for children. But the fiendish side of phosphorus had not been fully expressed until the Second World War when phosphorus bombs were used against civilian targets. In July 1943 an attack designed to destroy Hamburg (ironically the city of the discovery of phosphorus) was planned, Operation Gomorrah. Bombings continued for more than a week, in the midst of which a firestorm was set off. According to Emsley:

> At the end of that week 25 square kilometers (10 square miles) of the city were reduced to rubble and 800,000 people were homeless. ... The total number of civilians killed ... was 37,000, but 10,000 were missing, presumed dead. This can be compared with the 30,000 killed by bombs in London during the years 1940–45 but falls far short of the 80,000 who died in an incendiary raid on Tokyo by the USAF on the night of 9 March 1945; or the 140,000 who died when an atomic bomb was dropped on Hiroshima.[33]

The compensatory qualities of phosphorus, the demonic light in the darkness, more than offsets the imaginings of it as the source of all healing, the philosopher's stone. While positive and negative aspects of phosphorus could be further elaborated, I will simply note that Emsley also points out how nature seems to respond to such catastrophes as the destruction of Hamburg in "strange" ways. In this case, "in the autumn of 1943 the many lilac and chestnut trees of the city suddenly came into blossom as if it were spring."[34]

The timing of the discovery of phosphorus, the involvement of Leibniz in the story (recall he was identified by Jung as the key precursor to the idea of synchronicity), and the historical unfolding of the use of the element act as a "mirror" reflecting a dark genius in various ages, pointing to the objective psyche at play through the human use of this element. We could look at the ongoing story as a series of discrete synchronicities, often with a dark tone, or in the language of this text as a profound unfolding of an emergent process across several centuries. I would suggest that the latter framing broadens the notion of synchronicity beyond the moment of initial occurrence of a meaningful coincidence to include extensions of emergent events throughout a protracted period of time, not based on or reducible to simple cause and effect. We cannot predict the specific time course of an emergence but can become sensitive to its various manifestations and attempt to assess events along the trajectory of the emergent process, treating it as a field phenomenon rather than analyzing pieces of it reductively into discrete episodes. Obviously, there are dangers in this, as any cut-off point can be arbitrary, I would just encourage those interested in these phenomena to try and look more holistically at the patterns we are in. Previously, I attempted a limited version of this when I published some work on enactments that began with the time frame of an analytic day, rather than an individual clinical vignette.[35] This is an area that could benefit from further exploration and development.

## Serendipity

To conclude these reflections on events that reveal coincidences having consequences and meanings that go beyond the personal, I turn to a topic recognized in scientific and medical research, serendipity. The origins of the term *serendipity* are a bit exotic and unconsciously compensatory: it was coined in 1754 during the height of colonialism, in the Age of Enlightenment by a British man of letters, Horace Walpole, who also wrote gothic novels—a psychologically complex figure. The definition of serendipity offered by Walpole derives from the behavior of heroes of a tale he recalled from his childhood. These heroes as they traveled "were always making discoveries, by accidents and sagacity, of things which they were not in quest of."[36] It is the gift or capacity of the well-informed mind that is open to chance that can make the curious or odd, often seemingly minor occurrence in an encounter into a meaningful, at time momentous, event, that is, for the synchronistic dimension to become more evident.

The tale Walpole drew upon for his neologism was one that by the time it was first published in Europe in Venice in 1557 (called the *Peregrinaggio*), had already traveled far, previously having been translated from Persian into Italian. In English it has become known as "The Three Princes of Serendip," where Serendip refers to the name of the island the princes are from, sometimes called Sarandib or Simhaladvipa, more commonly known in the West as Ceylon, now Sri Lanka. Thus it is a concept that from a Western European or American perspective is imbued with otherness; it imports a notion not directly available to Western thought and was even somewhat ridiculed by Walpole himself for its "childish" origins. However, not all lucky accidents are synchronicities with meaningful coincidences, especially of an acausal nature.[37] It often takes some time and research to discern whether or not a serendipitous occurrence includes a synchronicity. I will give one example where this is likely the case, the discovery of penicillin.

The first of the key researchers in this story is Alexander Fleming, a Scottish bacteriologist who had witnessed the horror of tremendous numbers of deaths due to infections in soldiers of World War I. From this he resolved to find chemical agents that could kill the deadly microbes.[38] A pathway began to open in November of 1921 when he had a cold and a drop of mucous from his runny nose fell into a colony of benign bacteria and dissolved them. Recognizing a potential antimicrobial agent he went on to discover lysozyme (an element in the body's natural defense system, though not effective against the disease agents under consideration); for details see the work of Morton Meyers, a radiologist from SUNY Stony Brook.[39] Because of his own desultory and self-deprecating style Fleming's discovery went almost unnoticed.

Starting in the summer of 1928, however, Fleming was involved in what has been called "an incredible chain of fortunate circumstance."[40] He had a penchant for working with bacteria that had distinct colors, so as to play with patterns and to note changes. In this case the key colony of bacteria was in a petri dish on a pile of such dishes slated to be disinfected when Fleming chose one at random to show his assistant. He had picked one contaminated by a mold, not in itself unusual, but he did notice that there was a region around the mold that was free of bacteria (known as a "halo of inhibition"). He recognized the significance even though he had never seen a disease-causing bacteria destroyed due to proximity to a mold. He had learned to cultivate a curiosity for the unexpected even when occurring in seemingly trivial circumstance—an attitude that can be quite useful in attending to unconscious material in general and synchronicities in particular.

Looking in greater detail at the story, the mold that destroyed the bacteria was extremely rare (samples were being grown in the same building on the floor below Fleming's laboratory in attempts to find ways to desensitize people with asthma). The spores entered Fleming's petri dish at a critical moment, just as he was implanting the staphylococci bacteria—any later time and the bacteria would have been able to overwhelm the spores. In addition, the mold only works on colonies that are just beginning to multiply. There had been a heat wave in London that broke the day Fleming inoculated the petri dish—had this not happened the higher heat would have suppressed the mold relative to the bacteria—then the weather warmed up again. As Fleming's colleague Ronald Hare found, these were the *only* conditions and sequence of conditions that would have allowed the discovery to be made.[41] For reasons that are not wholly evident, Fleming did not go on to try his "mold juice" as a drug. However, he did preserve the mold strain. It now turned to others to make the discovery into a medical miracle, and again some rather amazing serendipity was at play.

A group of researchers at Oxford, Florey (an Australian pathologist), Chain (a Jewish biochemist refugee from Hitler's Germany), and Heatley (a biochemist), were instrumental in moving the story on. Studying the way cell walls could be dissolved they drew on Fleming's earlier work on lysozyme and on the penicillin mold largely because they had a culture of this mold in their building. They were not looking for an antimicrobial drug but wanted to isolate an enzyme on the surface of bacteria; it was purely scientific research without a biomedical focus. As with Fleming a series of lucky choices brought their attention to the potential benefits of the mold, and by 1940 as the war was underway in Europe they had their first evidence. And, because of the war they could not create adequate supplies of the penicillin-containing mold extract so Florey and Heatley went to the United States with their precious mold at the end of June 1941. The U.S. government was pleased to assist them and referred them to a research center of the Department of Agriculture in Peoria, Illinois because of its large fermentation labs. As the head of the fermentation division, Robert Coghill, noted, theirs was "the only laboratory where the corn steep liquor magic would have been discovered"[42]—corn steep liquor was a nutrient upon which the mold thrived and was available in vast quantities, allowing yields far in excess of what had been achieved at Oxford.

As the United States entered the war, the interest in this project grew; military units around the world were sending in mold samples in the hopes of finding molds that produced the highest quantities of penicillin. According to Meyers:

> In the end, the army was beaten by Mary Hunt, a laboratory aide who one day brought in a yellow mold she had discovered growing on a rotten cantaloupe at a fruit market right in Peoria. This proved to be *Penicillium chrysogenum,* a strain that produced 3,000 times more penicillin than Fleming's original mold! This made commercial production of penicillin feasible.[43]

By 1943 clinical trials had proven the effectiveness of penicillin in treating gram-positive bacteria, so the U.S. army began trials. By the time of D-Day (June 1944) U.S. drug manufacturers were producing sufficient penicillin to treat all of the wounded. This was to have a powerful, even decisive impact on the course of the war. After the war the drug became commercially available and deaths by bacterial infections dropped dramatically. In 1945 Fleming together with Florey and Chain shared the Nobel Prize for medicine; Heatley was not fully recognized until 1990 when he was given an honorary MD from Oxford.[44]

As serendipity has become acceptable as a part of scientific discovery, the numbers of incidents of it being reported and found in the historical record have grown. Now there are books devoted to the topic, and it has its own entry in Wikipedia with long lists of examples in many fields (chemistry, pharmacology, medicine and biology, physics and astronomy, inventions, etc.). Similarly, Ernest Jones saw in Freud's *Interpretation of Dreams* a "perfect example of serendipity, for the discovery of what dreams mean was made quite incidentally—one might almost say accidentally—when Freud was engaged in exploring the meaning of the psychoneuroses."[45] Jung went on to see meaning in the serendipitous that opened up new areas of exploration through his theory of synchronicity.

A final relevant example is drawn from the research presented in the previous chapter, the serendipitous discovery of mirror neurons. Iacoboni relates the lore around how the initial discovery that a select group of neurons in the premotor cortex were unexpectedly observed to fire when macaque monkeys were observing someone in the lab eating, while at the time these neurons were only expected to fire as a part of action on the monkey's part.[46] Everyone seems agreed on the general sequence of events leading to the discovery, but no one recalls the exact actions taken or who was eating what food at the time it happened; it has a dreamlike or mythic quality about it. The impact of mirror neurons upon our understanding of how we are linked to one another and other creatures and even the objects of our world has been tremendous. Perhaps the retrospective creation of an urban legend here reflects the human tendency to create narratives around synchronistic or emergent events, rendering them mythic—I would suggest the early twenty-first century has become a time of brain mythology with neuroscientific verification of the archetypal truths.

Whether serendipities are truly synchronistic or have a synchronistic core can be debated, even in Jungian circles, because of the question of attribution of meaning. As with the penicillin case, the meaningfulness of each of the coincidences does not always have an immediate link to a psychic state, especially of the researcher(s). However, when seen against the backdrop of a larger cultural narrative, the emergence of meaning can become staggering. Therefore I suggest that a modeling of such events within the complexity paradigm actually helps us detect the self-organizing features that only manifest as the human narrative capacity is brought into play. Synchronicity then is broadened to that aspect of our narrative truth that is not based on cause and effect rationality but reveals itself through the emergence of self-organizing features that evoke a feeling of surprise, from curiously mild serendipities to stunning coincidences of great significance.

# Afterword

To better grasp the idea of synchronicity I have found myself exploring, at times feeling compelled by the material into new areas beyond the clinical domain where I am most comfortable, yet it has also been deeply moving and exciting. The encounter has had its impact, at times like the wounding angel Jacob wrestled for a night. Initially I had thought I would bring my scientific background to bear on a psychological topic, but in the end I find that my views of science have been at least equally transformed as a result of this work, as is likely to occur in an analytic process.

By locating Jung's thinking within the frame of the scientific discoveries and controversies occurring within his lifetime, it has become more apparent to me that he was profoundly engaged by this discourse, even if he did not read or fully comprehend all the contemporary developments in science. His psychological acumen seems to have allowed him to resonate with what was active in the collective. His intuitions about principles of psychic ordering and organizing involved in acts of creation in time, to be placed on an equivalent footing with space, time, and causality, have truly radical significance that I believe has yet to be adequately appreciated. In the light of modern cosmology I have come to see this insight as identifying the organizing principle that is at the origins of the appearance of space, time, light, and matter, and in fact is behind every major originary event in our world. I believe this is what Jung was pointing to with his use of the term *psychoid;* it refers to the capacity or propensity for organization that emerged out of the hypothesized singularity (from which came the Big Bang), the origin point of our universe. The self-organization implicit in the psychoid is thereby linked to synchronicity; in consequence the psychoid would hold the principle that has allowed the emergence of everything, including the mind and soul. That there are enormous philosophical, theological, as well as scientific consequences that derive from this view is beginning to be appreciated, though Jung's foresight in this is a well-kept secret.

Tracing some of the scientific roots of Jung's ideas has helped to better locate this dimension of his thinking, which stems from the tradition of *Naturphilosophie* and holism. Although Jung's grasp of field theory tended to lean backward to the classical models of the nineteenth century, with the help of Pauli and Einstein his intuition sought and at times grasped relativistic vistas. This is another area that could yield much for analytical psychology if explored further, both theoretically and clinically. By including the importance of symmetry breaking as an essential aspect of emergence, a more detailed understanding of interactions in the clinical field may be possible. Learning to identify and engage with moments of complexity as they constellate would give increased flexibility to clinicians. Similarly, understanding the fears of, anxieties about, and defenses against emergent processes could offer enhanced containment and metabolism of the resistances to needed transformations and facilitate individuation. The importance of symmetry, symmetry breaking, and asymmetry in human development is an area of great potential; the study of the process of identity formation as well as the discoveries of agency throughout the life cycle will be powerfully augmented by such work. All of these areas could draw upon a more fully articulated theory of synchronicity as emergence.

As the examination of empathy gives substance to multiple levels of interactions in the analytic field (affective, cognitive, conscious, and unconscious) the question of unconscious communication comes to the fore. In the context of clinical studies of synchronicity, I have suggested a range of intensities of synchronistic phenomena linked to frequency of occurrence and to types of interactions based on levels of disturbance of or elements of genius in the psyche.[1] Once a spectrum of synchronicities is envisioned, we can imagine a layering of levels of depth in phenomena, including those of empathy, resonance, enactments, projective identifications, psychosomatic events, and unconscious communications generally, as well as overt synchronicities, all likely having synchronistic cores. Outside the Jungian community the synchronistic dimensions of these phenomena have received scant attention. However, as an atmosphere of increased transparency enters discussions of clinical data, especially the inclusion of details of countertransference and field experiences, more reports of "anomalous phenomena" are being published. At the same time neuroscientific studies are providing insights into some experiences that were unexplainable in the past; clearly this is an area of rapid, mobile development that will continue to explore provocative topics of interest to those who are fascinated by synchronicity.

While Jung articulated the theory of the collective unconscious, composed of archetypal patterns, the sociocultural ramifications of the theory are only beginning to be examined, such as in discussions about cultural complexes. In this book I have built upon several articles to begin to construct a network theory of the collective unconscious; I believe this deserves fuller study with explorations of various aspects of large group psychology, as well as applications of network theory, to our ideas about individuation. As a step in that direction I have sought to raise the possibility of looking at the historical record in various fields for synchronistic phenomena that may have occurred at the interface of cultures and/or across time frames beyond the individual.

Recognizing that synchronicity might stem from a postcolonial worldview does not mean that Jung personally completed such a transformation. Rather, my suggestion is that Jung's visionary concept when put against a postcolonial background reveals more of its radical nature for political discourse. This viewpoint as well as the concept itself could be refined through dialogue with those who work from such a perspective. As an idea that emerged at the cusp of a world in transition, I believe it has not been taken far enough from its nascent state, but the time for reassessment and extension may be at hand.

The political dimensions of synchronicity are challenging to envision and comment upon in a meaningful way that would also respect the psychological integrity of multiple perspectives necessarily involved.

Yet, leadership that ignores the *kairos* of events can quickly get out of sync with the people it is meant to represent and guide. The application of synchronicity to arenas outside the clinical is another new development that will require time and contributions from people in various disciplines if it is to help us understand our collective experiences in a deeper way.

In conclusion, the image of the mirror, or "mirroring," has been a leitmotif through the chapters of this book. From the psychology of key individuals such as Pauli's mirror complex, or Jung's struggle with this in the symmetry-breaking aspect of diagram of the self, to fundamental aspects of the universe, for example, parity laws and their violations, or to the roots of consciousness in empathy grounded in mirror neurons and even to cultural mirrors, the reflective process has informed our thinking. While the symbology of the mirror is a topic with its own literature beyond the current scope, I am suggesting that synchronicity with its notion of equivalence (of the physical and the psychological) offers a new dimension to what mirroring is and how we experience it. Hopefully we will learn to reflect more deeply through our experiences and understandings of the interconnectedness of our world as mirrored through synchronicity.

# Notes

## Foreword

1. D. Rosen and J. Weishaus (2004). *The Healing Spirit of Haiku.* Berkeley, CA: North Atlantic Books, 28–30.

2. J. Beebe (2008). "Objective Sympathy." Keynote address at the conference Beyond Ego Psychology: Journeys of the Heart East and West. Kyoto, Japan, April 11, 2008. Unpublished paper.

3. Ibid.

4. J. Kerwin. Personal communication, November 2008.

## Introduction

1. Jung, "Synchronicity: An Acausal Connecting Principle," 10.

2. Jung and Pauli, *The Interpretation of Nature and the Psyche.*

3. Meier, *Atom and Archetype.*

4. Cambray, "Synchronicity and Emergence."

## Chapter 1

1. Mayer, *Extraordinary Knowing,* 14.

2. Ibid., 16.

3. Mayer, "Freud and Jung," 2002.

4. Jung, "Synchronicity," paragraphs 843 and 982.

5. Jung, *Dream Analysis,* ed. W. M. McGuire.

6. Ibid., 44.

7. Ibid., 44–45.

8. Ibid., 417.

9. "Richard Wilhelm: In Memoriam," paragraph 81.

10. Jung and Pauli, *Interpretation of Nature and the Psyche*.

11. Meier, *Atom and Archetype*.

12. Ibid.

13. Gieser, *The Innermost Kernel*.

14. Jung, "Synchronicity," 3.

15. Ibid., 5; Computer scientist/philosopher John Sowa (2000; http://www
.jfsowa.com/ontology/causal.htm, accessed 27 October 2007) cites physicist
Max Born's *Natural Philosophy of Cause and Chance* (1949) regarding three
assumptions that dominated physics until the twentieth century:

(i) "*Causality* postulates that there are laws by which the occurrence of an
entity B of a certain class depends on the occurrence of an entity A of another
class, where the word *entity* means any physical object, phenomenon, situation, or event. A is called the cause, B the effect."

(ii) "*Antecedence* postulates that the cause must be prior to, or at least
simultaneous with, the effect."

(iii) "*Contiguity* postulates that cause and effect must be in spatial contact
or connected by a chain of intermediate things in contact."

In considering the shift necessitated by relativity and quantum mechanics,
Born is quoted as concluding that "chance has become the primary notion,
mechanics an expression of its quantitative laws, and the overwhelming evidence of causality with all its attributes in the realm of ordinary experience
is satisfactorily explained by the statistical laws of large numbers." Although
Born would retain classical causality for events on the human scale, the
required shifts at the most fundamental levels have generated philosophical
debate and divergence among professionals.

16. Ibid., 7.

17. Ibid., 9.

18. For a more detailed discussion of Kammerer's ideas and his tragic fate
see Koestler's *The Case of the Midwife Toad*.

19. Jung, "Synchronicity," 11.

20. Meier, *Atom and Archetype*, letter 37 P, 28 June 1949.

21. Ibid.

22. Charet, *Spiritualism and the Foundations of C. G. Jung's Psychology*.

23. Main, *The Rupture of Time*.

24. Tart, "Causality and Synchronicity," 121.

25. Jung, "Synchronicity," 19.

26. Cambray, "Synchronicity and Emergence."

27. See Diaconsis and Moesteller, "Methods for Studying Coincidences."

28. Meier, *Atom and Archetype,* letter 45 P, 24 November 1950.

29. Ibid., 28; emphasis in original.

30. Main, *The Rupture of Time,* 44–47.

31. Meier, *Atom and Archetype,* letter 37 P, 28 June 1949, 38.

32. Ibid., letter 37 P, 28 June 1949.

33. Driesch, *The Science and Philosophy of the Organism,* 83.

34. Jung, in "On the Nature of the Psyche," paragraphs 367–68.

35. Jung, "Synchronicity," 20.

36. Ibid., 30.

37. McGuire, *The Freud/Jung Letters,* letter to Freud, 230 J.

38. Jung, *Letters,* letter 25 February 1953.

39. Jung, "Synchronicity," 24.

40. Singh, *Big Bang,* 152.

41. In a feat of literary intuition Edgar Allan Poe already anticipated the Big Bang cosmology with his 1848 essay "Eureka: A Prose Poem." In this he imagines a "primal particle" from which the universe unfolds; his view employs "divine volition." This work is available online, see http://www.text log.de/poe-eureka.html.

42. Singh, *Big Bang,* 160.

43. Ibid., 273.

44. Ibid., 276.

45. Ibid., 314.

46. Jung, "Flying Saucers," paragraph 810.

47. Hannah, *Jung: His Life and Work,* 338.

48. Hoyle, *The Black Cloud.*

49. Jung, "Flying Saucers," paragraphs 810–15.

50. Jung, *Letters,* 407.

51. Italics in original; Meier, *Atom and Archetype,* letter 54 P, 73.

52. Jung, *Letters,* 118.

53. Jung, "Synchronicity," 29–30.

54. Jung, *Letters* 494–95.

55. Nichol, *The Essential David Bohm.*

56. Jung, "Synchronicity," 102, n. 17.

57. Main, *The Rupture of Time* and *Revelations of Chance.*

58. Main, *The Rupture of Time.*

59. Jung, "Synchronicity," 33.

60. Jung, "Foreword to the 'I Ching.'"

61. Jung, "Synchronicity," 36, italics in the original.

62. Ibid., 70.

63. Ibid., 71.

64. Cirlot, *A Dictionary of Symbols,* 62.

65. Jung, "Synchronicity," 73, n. 13.

66. Jung, "On the Nature of Dreams," paragraph 545.

67. Jung, "Synchronicity," 74.

68. Quoted in Jung, "Synchronicity," 83.

69. Quoted in Broad, *Leibniz: An Introduction,* 124; italics in the original.

70. Jung, "Synchronicity," 84, n. 70.

71. Cambray, "The Place of the 17th Century in Jung's Encounter with China."

72. Kim, *Supervenience and Mind,* 135.

73. See Cambray, "The Place of the 17th Century in Jung's Encounter with China."

74. Reproduced in ibid., 203.

75. Wilhelm, "Leibniz and the *I-Ching.*"

76. In Campbell, ed., *Man and Time,* 207.

77. Jung, "Synchronicity," 90.

78. Ibid., 94.

79. See Ehrsson, "The Experimental Induction of Out-of-Body Experiences."

80. Frisch, *The Dancing Bees.*

81. Jung, "Synchronicity," 99; emphasis in the original.

82. Gieser, *The Innermost Kernel,* 290.

83. Jung, "Problems of Modern Psychotherapy," paragraph 163.

84. Cambray, "Synchronicity and Emergence."

## *Chapter 2*

1. Aziz, *C. G. Jung's Psychology of Religion and Synchronicity;* Bishop, *Synchronicity and Intellectual Intuition;* Combs and Holland, *Synchronicity:*

*Science, Myth, and the Trickster;* Eisold, "Jung, Jungians, and Psychoanalysis;" Hoepke, *There Are No Accidents;* Main, *Encountering Jung;* Main, *The Rupture of Time;* Main, *Revelations of Chance;* Mansfield, *Synchronicity, Science, and Soul-Making;* Mayer, "Freud and Jung"; Peat, *Synchronicity: The Bridge between Matter and Mind;* von Franz, *Number and Time;* von Franz, *On Divination and Synchronicity;* von Franz, *Psyche and Matter;* among others.

2. Aristotle, *Metaphysics,* Book VIII, section 6.

3. Jung, "A Study in the Process of Individuation."

4. In Jung, *Psychology and Alchemy*—scholars have identified these as Wolfgang Pauli's dreams.

5. Jung, *Two Essays on Analytical Psychology.*

6. Wiktionary, http://en.wiktionary.org/wiki/.

7. Early development of the self was not adequately articulated by Jung; he left this to Freud and others while focusing on adult development. Fordham constructed a theory of the self that was consistent and congruent with Jung's ideas but included psychoanalytically informed models as well as his own creative formulations. E. Neumann offered a mythopoetic theory of development along traditional Jungian lines (e.g., his 1954 *Origins and History of Consciousness*); also, see Samuels (1985, pp. 155–59) for a comparison of these two developmental theories.

8. Jung, "The Psychology of the Child Archetype," paragraph 302. Quoted and discussed in Cambray and Carter, *Analytical Psychology,* 119.

9. Samuels, Shorter, and Plaut, *A Critical Dictionary of Jungian Analysis,* 27.

10. Jung, "On Psychological Understanding," paragraphs 412–14.

11. Ibid., paragraph 399.

12. Dobbs, *The Foundation of Newton's Alchemy;* Dobbs, *The Janus Faces of Genius.*

13. Cambray, "Emergence and the Self."

14. Yates, *The Art of Memory.*

15. Agassi, "Leibniz's Place in the History of Physics."

16. Damasio, *Looking for Spinoza.*

17. The reductive paradigm developed momentum and held sway through much of the eighteenth century, in sync with Enlightenment mentality. Holism was largely marginalized, at least historically; there were alternative approaches to science, e.g., Gabriel Venel's championing chemistry based on

apprenticeship, highlighting experience both sensory and intuitive, versus Lavoisier's sense of experimentation and mass training in scientific technique. Chertok and Stengers (in *A Critique of Psychoanalytic Reason*) detail how the scientific worldview informed Freud, who emulated Lavoisier in many ways; Jung's methodology, therefore, would be more in line with the holistic approaches in contradistinction to Freud.

18. Cantor, Gooding, and James, *Michael Faraday*, 77.

19. In Williams, *The Origins of Field Theory*, 118.

20. As a first approximation and visual aid, imagine a bowling ball on a trampoline, the weight of the ball will cause the flat sheet of the trampoline to "warp" around it, curving the surface so that if a marble were placed in its vicinity it would roll toward the ball along the curvature, analogously massive objects warp the gravitational field of space-time.

21. In *The Varieties of Religious Experience*, from James's Gifford Lectures of 1901–2, he writes: "The expression 'field of consciousness' has but recently come into vogue in the psychology books. Until quite lately the unit of mental life which figured most was the single 'idea,' supposed to be a definitely outlined thing. But at present psychologists are tending, first, to admit that the actual unit is more probably the total mental state, the entire wave of consciousness or field of objects present to thought at any time; and, second, to see that it is impossible to outline this wave, this field, with any definiteness. . . . The important fact which this 'field' formula commemorates is the indetermination of the margin. Inattentively realized as is the matter which the margin contains, it is nevertheless there, and helps both to guide our behavior and to determine the next movement of our attention. It lies around us like a 'magnetic field,' inside of which our centre of energy turns like a compass-needle, as the present phase of consciousness alters into its successor" (James, *The Varieties of Religious Experience*, 190–91).

James is obviously drawing on the physics we have been discussing here and curiously is intuiting aspects of indeterminacy found in quantum theory as well as the more obvious parallel with unconscious phenomena. However, the model of the field that James uses is drawn from classical field theory. Robert Richardson (2006) in a recent biography of James notes: "In 1875 he was reading in modern physics as well. James Clerk Maxwell had become in 1871 the first professor of experimental physics at Cambridge University in England. In 1873 he brought out his *Treatise on Electricity and Magnetism*.

In May 1875 James read and reviewed a book called *The Unseen Universe,* by the physicist and mathematician Peter Guthrie Tait . . . and the physicist and meteorologist Balfour Stewart." While Jung's model has elements from both classical and relativistic field theories, Gieser (*The Innermost Kernel*) has shown that Pauli objected to Jung's way of formulating the unconscious and even compared it with the classical field concepts and Maxwell's equations, noting that Jung did not adequately include "the new epistemological situation revealed by quantum physics . . . he still had a tendency to treat the unconscious as a field that may be observed without considering the influence of the observation" (p. 245).

22. Jung, *Letters,* 109.

23. Italics in original; Gieser, *The Innermost Kernel,* 244–45.

24. Cambray and Carter, *Analytical Psychology,* 126–28.

25. Mumford, Series, and Wright, *Indra's Pearls,* ii.

## *Chapter 3*

1. Cambray, "Synchronicity and Emergence"; Cambray, "Towards the Feeling of Emergence"; and Cambray, "Emergence and the Self."

2. Some authors argue for a nuanced differentiation of holism from emergentism. For one discussion of the various ways these concepts have been used see Sawyer, *Social Emergence,* chapter 2, "The History of Emergence."

3. Gleick, *Chaos,* chapter 1.

4. Cambray, "Synchronicity and Emergence." 411–14.

5. Camazine et al., *Self-Organization in Biological Systems.*

6. Freud, *New Introductory Lectures on Psycho-Analysis,* 55.

7. Ibid.

8. The inaugural work of Tresan, "Jungian Metapsychology and Neurobiological Theory"; and an important contribution by Saunders and Skar, "Archetypes, Complexes, and Self-Organization"; and Knox, *How Does Analysis Cure?;* Wilkinson, *Coming into Mind;* McDowell, "Principle of Organization"; Martin-Vallas, "The Transferential Chimera: A Clinical Approach" and "The Transferential Chimera: Some Theoretical Considerations"; and Solomon, *The Self in Transformation.*

9. Cambray and Carter, *Analytical Psychology.*

10. Cowan, *Barcelona 2004.*

11. Morowitz, *The Emergence of Everything;* Clayton, *Mind and Emergence.*

12. Cambray and Carter, *Analytical Psychology.*

13. Jacobi, *The Psychology of C. G. Jung,* 85–88.

14. Edinger, *Anatomy of the Psyche.*

15. Csermely, *Weak Links.*

16. Cambray, "Emergence and the Self."

17. Mainzer, *Symmetry and Complexity.*

18. Merriam Webster online dictionary, 15 December 2007.

19. Brading and Castellani, "Symmetry and Symmetry Breaking."

20. In Eckermann, *Conversations of Goethe with Johann Peter Eckermann,* letter to Eckermann, 23 March 1829.

21. Ramachandran, *A Brief Tour of Human Consciousness,* 16–17.

22. Thornhill and Gangestad, "The Scent of Symmetry," 175.

23. Reported by Thornhill in Keil and Wilson, eds., *The MIT Encyclopedia of the Cognitive Sciences,* 752.

24. See Schattschneider, *M. C. Escher,* in passing.

25. Accessed 1 November 2008.

26. Wilford, "In Medieval Architecture, Signs of Advanced Math."

27. *New York Times,* 16 January 1957.

28. Meier, *Atom and Archetype,* 224.

29. Written to Victor Weisskopf, quoted in Gieser, *The Innermost Kernel,* 325.

30. Meier, *Atom and Archetype,* 76 P, p. 163.

31. Ibid., 165.

32. Ibid.

33. Ibid.

34. The remaining letters from Jung's side are penned by Aniela Jaffé.

35. Meier, *Atom and Archetype,* 76 P, p. 167.

36. Ibid., 168.

37. Ibid., 169.

38. Lammers, "Jung and White and the God of Terrible Double Aspect."

39. Lammers and Cunningham, eds., *The Jung-White Letters.*

40. Edinger, *The Aion Lectures.*

41. Jung, *Aion: Researches into the Phenomenology of the Self,* paragraph 409.

42. Lammers, "Jung and White and the God of Terrible Double Aspect."

43. Lammers and Cunningham, eds., *The Jung-White Letters.*

44. For an discussion of phase transitions in manifestations of the self see Hogenson, "The Self, the Symbolic, and Synchronicity"; for more a general scientific discussion see Mainzer, *Symmetry and Complexity*—as an example consider the sharp melting points of many crystalline solids: as the temperature is slowly raised to being at or just over this point a rapid change of state from solid to liquid occurs.

45. From Wikipedia.

46. Quote in Cambray, "Synchronicity and Emergence," 426.

47. Brading and Castellani, "Symmetry and Symmetry Breaking."

## Chapter 4

1. Cambray, "Synchronicity and Emergence."

2. Needham, *Science and Civilisation in China,* Vol. 2, *History of Scientific Thought,* 304.

3. Jung, "Foreword to the 'I Ching,'" paragraphs 971–74.

4. Waltham, *Chuang Tzu,* 110.

5. Ibid., 157.

6. Vischer, *Uber das optische Formgefuhl.*

7. Titchener, *A Textbook of Psychology.*

8. For selected examples see Lipps, "Aesthetische Einfühlung," "Einfhlung, innere Nachahmung, und Organempfindungen," "Weiteres zur Einfühlung," "Aesthetik," and "Zur Einfühlung."

9. For a discussion of Lipps's influence on Freud see Pigman, "Freud and the History of Empathy."

10. Jung, *Psychological Types,* paragraph 486, my italics.

11. Kohut, *How Does Analysis Cure?* 82.

12. Jung, "Synchronicity: An Acausal Connecting Principle," paragraph 958.

13. A variety of electromagnetic scanning techniques have been employed in addition to fMRI, for example, positron emission tomography (PET), magnetoencephalography (MEG), transcranial magnetic stimulation (TMS), as well as the older technique of electroencephalography (EEG) have all helped to contribute to the rapidly growing neuroscientific understanding of the brain and its functioning.

14. Hatfield, Cacioppo, and Rapson, *Emotional Contagion.*

15. Chartrand and Bargh, "The Chameleon Effect."

16. Van Baaren et al., "Mimicry and Pro-Social Behavior," 71.

17. Iacoboni, *Mirroring People,* 268–72.

18. Decety, "A Social Cognitive Neuroscience Model of Human Empathy," 247.

19. Iacoboni, *Mirroring People,* 66.

20. Ibid., 68.

21. Wimmer and Perner, "Beliefs about Beliefs."

22. Morell, "Inside Animal Minds."

23. Decety, "A Social Cognitive Neuroscience Model of Human Empathy."

24. Fogassi and Gallese, "The Neural Correlates of Action Understanding in Non-Human Primates," 15.

25. Gallese, Fadiga, Fogassi, and Rizzolatti, "Action Recognition in the Premotor Cortex."

26. Rizzolatti, Craighero, and Fadiga, "The Mirror System in Humans."

27. Singer, Seymour, O'Doherty, Kaube, Dolan, and Frith, "Empathy for Pain Involves the Affect but Not Sensory Components of Pain"; Avenanti, Bueti, Galati, and Aglioti, "Transcranial Magnetic Stimulation Highlights the Sensorimotor Side of Empathy for Pain"; Singer and Frith, "The Painful Side of Empathy."

28. Fogassi and Gallese, "The Neural Correlates of Action Understanding in Non-Human Primates."

29. Iacoboni, *Mirroring People.*

30. Ibid., 25.

31. Ibid.

32. Ibid., 26.

33. Ibid., 202.

34. Ibid., 203.

35. Ibid., 144.

36. Ibid., 162.

37. In *Collected Works 5,* paragraph 11 Jung references James and Lotze in the same sentence (paragraph 11, n. 3 and n. 4) where Jung is discussing directed or logical thinking as being adapted to reality "by means of which we imitate the successiveness of objectively real things, so that the images

inside our mind follow one another in the same strictly causal sequence as the events taking place outside it," which he ties directly to Lotze's 1874 book *Logik* (p. 58).

38. Iacoboni, *Mirroring People*, 58.

39. Grotowski, *Towards a Poor Theatre.*

40. Goldman, *Simulating Minds.* Because of the richly textured, complex arguments developed in this book, no attempt will be made to summarize contents, but those interested in this area will find it highly rewarding. Iacoboni praises Goldman's work in passing (Iacoboni, *Mirroring People,* 17) and discusses some of Goldman's collaborative work with Vittorio Gallese (ibid., 33–34).

41. Goldman, "Imitation, Mind Reading, and Simulation."

42. For example, see Sandler, "Countertransference and Role-Responsiveness."

43. Iacoboni, *Mirroring People*, 174–83.

44. Schwartz-Salant, *The Borderline Personality.*

45. Prinz, "Imitation and Moral Development," 278.

46. Ibid., 282.

47. Huesmann, "Imitation and the Effects of Observing Media Violence on Behavior."

48. Iacoboni, *Mirroring People,* 214–18.

49. The research on mirror neurons has brought philosophical issues into focus that bears directly on this point. Iacoboni postulates an "existential neuroscience" in which he urges us "to be suspicious of rigid dichotomies" as these brain cells "show that we are not alone, but are biologically wired and evolutionarily designed to be deeply interconnected with one another" (*Mirroring People,* 267). Jung's tendency to present psychological data in terms of bipolar opposites requires a revision of his theories and methods when this bipolarity is found to be in conflict with observations.

50. Cook, *Hua-yen Buddhism.*

51. Mumford, Series, and Wright, *Indra's Pearls.*

52. Ibid., xviii.

53. De Bary and Bloom, *Sources of Chinese Tradition,* 474.

54. Jung, "The Psychology of the Transference."

55. Jacoby, *The Psychology of C. G. Jung.*

56. For a contemporary neuropsychoanalytic view, which is closer to the

Jungian perspective with emphasis on more interactive and less accusatory readings of the other as an active agent "putting" unwanted psychic contents "into" the analyst, see Greatrix, "Projective Identification: How Does It Work?"

57. At http://www.edge.org/documents/archive/edge69.html.

58. Ramachandran, *A Brief Tour of Human Consciousness*.

59. Cambray, "Reconsidering Imitation"; Iacoboni, *Mirroring People*, 47–52.

## Chapter 5

1. Cambray, "Democracy, Time, and Organizational Life in the International Jungian Community."

2. Meier, *The Greek Discovery of Politics*.

3. Csapo and Miller, "Democracy, Empire, and Art."

4. Ibid., 103.

5. Onians, *The Origins of European Thought about the Body, the Mind, the Soul, the World, Time, and Fate*.

6. Jung, *Civilization in Transition*, paragraph 585.

7. Von Franz, *Number and Time*, 44.

8. Ibid., 256.

9. Onians, *The Origins of European Thought about the Body, the Mind, the Soul, the World, Time, and Fate*, 211, n. 9.

10. Manville and Ober, *A Company of Citizens*.

11. Inaugurated by Solon in 594 BCE.

12. Meier, *The Greek Discovery of Politics*, 25.

13. While much of the initial research in this area was for military defensive purposes, the applications of studies on network resilience have been expanded to a very wide variety of systems (molecular, biological, financial, epidemiological, political, etc.). This thinking obviously can be extended to an analysis of psychological defenses, especially when a model such as Jung's on the structure of the psyche is used. The network of complexes and archetypes that make up the psyche in this model could be examined for the types of defenses operating in the various elements. The decrease or removal of these defenses through Jungian analysis would then be seen in enhanced integration of the psychological energy from these complexes into con-

sciousness. Similarly, the psychology of interpersonal relations would form a further level of complexity to such a model. A theory of individuation based on a network model is therefore possible but beyond the scope of this text.

14. For example, Cambray, "Synchronicity and Emergence."

15. Carrasco, *Quetzalcoatl and the Irony of Empire*, 150.

16. For a discussion of the use of this myth in psychotherapy with Mexican addicts, see Sutton, "Addiction: Between Paradise and Hell, the Challenge of Maintaining the Tensions."

17. Carrasco, *Quetzalcoatl and the Irony of Empire*, 148, for details.

18. Ibid., 200.

19. Nicholson, *Topiltzin Quetzalcoatl: The Once and Future Lord of the Toltecs*, 236–44.

20. A Google search using the keywords "Quetzalcoatl bearded images," yields a wealth of images that can be compared with those of Cortés.

21. Carrasco, *Quetzalcoatl and the Irony of Empire*, 196.

22. Ibid.

23. Ibid., 197.

24. Ibid., 208.

25. Aziz, *C. G. Jung's Psychology of Religion and Synchronicity*.

26. Bergland, "Toltec Mirrors," 143.

27. Carrasco, *Quetzalcoatl and the Irony of Empire*, 190.

28. Bergland, "Toltec Mirrors," 141.

29. There is an intense debate in the literature as to whether the Hawaiians actually saw Cook as an incarnation of Lono or not, see Obeyesekere, *The Apotheosis of Captain Cook*, and Sahlins, *How "Natives" Think*.

30. The discovery of phosphorus was depicted in a highly romanticized fashion in 1771 by the painter Joseph Wright in his work *The Alchymist, In Search of the Philosopher's Stone, Discovers Phosphorus, and Prays for the Successful Conclusion of His Operation, as Was the Custom of the Ancient Chymical Astrologers;* see http://www.geocities.com/jvertesi/wright/ for a detailed discussion of the man, the image, and its composition, in the article by Janet Vertesi, "Light and Enlightenment in Joseph Wright of Derby's *The Alchymist.*"

31. Emsley, *The 13th Element*, 5–24.

32. Ibid., 25–42.

33. Emsley, *The 13th Element*, 150.

34. Ibid., 153.

35. Cambray, "Enactments and Amplification."

36. Remer, *Serendipity and the Three Princes*, 6; emphasis added.

37. For an extended exploration of multiple dimensions of serendipity, including its origins, social history, its moral and political implications, as well as an understanding of its evolving role in science, see Merton and Barber, *The Travels and Adventures of Serendipity.*

38. The seductive pull of the synchronistic aspects of the penicillin story have generated some fascinating urban legends that should not be mistaken for actual events, though they are of real interest as "memes." One particularly compelling story of this genre is that of Fleming (or his father in some versions), who saved Winston Churchill from drowning as boy and then Churchill's father rewarded him with a first class education, which leads him to the discovery of penicillin, which was in turn used to again save Churchill's life when the drug was used to stem potentially fatal pneumonias during World War II. The apocryphal nature of the story has been noted and discussed in various places, including the Web site of the Churchill Center: http://www.winstonchurchill.org/i4a/pages/index.cfm%3Fpageid=102.

39. Meyers, *Happy Accidents*, 62.

40. Ibid., 63.

41. Ibid., 69.

42. Ibid., 75.

43. Ibid.

44. For his role see ibid., 79; chapter 5 of Meyers's book tells the story of penicillin.

45. Jones, *The Life and Work of Sigmund Freud*, 350.

46. Iacoboni, *Mirroring People*, 51–52.

## Afterword

1. Cambray, "Synchronicity and Emergence."

# Bibliography

Agassi, Joseph. (1969). "Leibniz's Place in the History of Physics." *Journal of the History of Ideas* 30: 331–44.

Avenanti, Alessio, Domenica Bueti, Gaspare Galati, and Salvatore M. Aglioti. (2005). "Transcranial Magnetic Stimulation Highlights the Sensorimotor Side of Empathy for Pain." *Nature Neuroscience* 8: 955–60.

Aziz, Robert. (1990). *C. G. Jung's Psychology of Religion and Synchronicity.* Albany: State University of New York Press.

Bergland, Renee. (2007 online; copyright 2005). "Toltec Mirrors: Europeans and Native Americans in Each Other's Eyes." In *A Companion to the Literatures of Colonial America,* edited by Susan Castillo and Ivy Schweitzer. Blackwell Companions to Literature and Culture. Oxford: Blackwell.

Bishop, Paul. (2000). *Synchronicity and Intellectual Intuition in Kant, Swedenborg, and Jung.* Lampeter, Ceredigion, Wales: Edwin Mellen Press.

Born, Max. (1949). *Natural Philosophy of Cause and Chance,* Dover Publications, New York.

Brading, Katherine, and Elaine Castellani. (2008). "Symmetry and Symmetry Breaking," in the *Stanford Encyclopedia of Philosophy.* Retrieved 5 October 2008 from http://stanford.library.usyd.edu.au/entries/symmetry-breaking/.

Broad, C. D. (1975). *Leibniz: An Introduction.* London and New York: Cambridge University Press.

Camazine, S., J.-L. Deneubourg, N. R. Franks, J. Sneyd, G. Theraulaz, and E. Bonabeau. (2001). *Self-Organization in Biological Systems.* Princeton, N.J.: Princeton University Press, 142–65.

Cambray, Joseph. (2001). "Enactments and Amplification." *Journal of Analytical Psychology* 46 (2): 275–303.

———. (2002). "Synchronicity and Emergence." *American Imago* 59 (4): 409–34.

———. (2005). "The Place of the 17th Century in Jung's Encounter with China." *Journal of Analytical Psychology* 50 (2): 195–207.

———. (2006). "Towards the Feeling of Emergence." *Journal of Analytical Psychology* 51 (1): 1–20.

———. (2007). "Reconsidering Imitation." In *Who Owns Jung?* edited by Ann Casement. London: Karnac.

———. (2008). "Democracy, Time, and Organizational Life in the International Jungian Community." *Quadrant* 38 (2): 35–45.

———. (2009). "Emergence and the Self." In *Jungian Psychoanalysis,* edited by Murray Stein. Chicago: Open Court (in press).

Cambray, Joseph, and Linda Carter. (2004). *Analytical Psychology: Contemporary Perspectives in Jungian Analysis.* Hove and New York: Brunner-Routledge.

Campbell, Joseph, ed. (1957). *Man and Time: Papers from the Eranos Yearbooks.* Bollingen Series XXX.3. Princeton, N.J.: Princeton University Press.

Cantor, Geoffrey, David Gooding, and Frank A. J. L. James (1991/1996). *Michael Faraday.* Atlantic Highlands, N.J.: Humanities Press.

Carrasco, David. (2000). *Quetzalcoatl and the Irony of Empire.* Boulder: University Press of Colorado.

Casement, Ann, and David Tacey, eds. (2006). *The Idea of the Numinous: Contemporary Jungian and Psychoanalytic Perspectives.* East Sussex and New York: Routledge.

Charet, F. X. (1993). *Spiritualism and the Foundations of C. G. Jung's Psychology,* Albany: State University of New York Press.

Chartrand, Tanya L., and John A. Bargh. (1999). "The Chameleon Effect: The Perception-Behavior Link and Social Interaction." *Journal of Personality and Social Psychology* 76 (6): 893–910.

Chertok, L., and I. Stengers. (1992). *A Critique of Psychoanalytic Reason.* Stanford, Calif.: Stanford University Press.

Cirlot, Juan E. (1971). *A Dictionary of Symbols,* 2nd ed. New York: Philosophical Library.

Clayton, Philip. (2004). *Mind and Emergence.* New York: Oxford University Press.

Combs, Allan, and Mark Holland. (1996). *Synchronicity: Science, Myth, and the Trickster.* New York: Marlowe.

Cook, Francis H. (1977). *Hua-yen Buddhism: The Jewel Net of Indra.* University Park: Pennsylvania State University Press.

Cowan, Lyn, ed. (2006). *Barcelona 2004, Edges of Experience: Memory and Emergence.* Proceedings of the Sixteenth International Congress for Analytical Psychology. Einsiedeln, Switzerland: Daimon Verlag.

Csapo, Eric, and Margaret Miller. (1998). "Democracy, Empire, and Art: Toward a Politics of Time and Narrative." In *Democracy, Empire, and the Arts in Fifth-Century Athens,* edited by Deborah Boedeker and Kurt A. Raaflaub, 87–125. Cambridge, Mass.: Harvard University Press.

Csermely, Peter. (2006). *Weak Links: Stabilizers of Complex Systems from Proteins to Social Networks.* Berlin, Heidelberg, New York: Springer-Verlag.

Damasio, Antonio. (2003). *Looking for Spinoza: Joy, Sorrow, and the Feeling Brain.* New York: Harcourt.

de Bary, William Theodore, and Irene Bloom. (1999). *Sources of Chinese Tradition,* Vol. 1, *From Earliest Times to 1600,* 2nd ed. New York: Columbia University Press.

Decety, Jean. (2007). "A Social Cognitive Neuroscience Model of Human Empathy." In *Social Neuroscience: Integrating Biological and Psychological Explanations of Social Behavior,* edited by Eddie Harmon-Jones and Piotr Winkielman, 246–70. New York and London: Guilford Press.

Diaconsis, Persi, and Frederick Moesteller. (1989). "Methods for Studying Coincidences." *Journal of the American Statistical Association* 84 (408): 853–61.

Dobbs, Betty Jo Teeter. (1975). *The Foundation of Newton's Alchemy: Or, The Hunting of the Greene Lyon.* Cambridge: Cambridge University Press.

———. (1991). *The Janus Faces of Genius: The Role of Alchemy in Newton's Thought.* Cambridge: Cambridge University Press.

Driesch, Hans. (1908). *The Science and Philosophy of the Organism.* London: Adam and Charles Black.

Dusek, Val. (1999). *The Holistic Inspirations of Physics.* New Brunswick, N.J.: Rutgers University Press.

Eckermann, Johann Peter. (1998). *Conversations of Goethe with Johann Peter Eckermann.* Translated by John Oxenford. Edited by J. K. Moorhead. Introduction by Havelock Ellis. Cambridge, MA: Da Capo Press.

Edinger, Edward. (1985). *Anatomy of the Psyche.* La Salle, IL: Open Court.

———. (1996). *The Aion Lectures.* Toronto: Inner City Books.

Ehrsson, H. Henrik. (2007). "The Experimental Induction of Out-of-Body Experiences." *Science* 317 (5841): 1048.

Einstein, Albert. (1905). "Zur Elektrodynamik bewegter Körper." *Annalen der Physik* 17: 891–921.

———. (1915). "Die Feldgleichungen der Gravitation." Sitzungsberichte der Preussischen Akademie der Wissenschaften zu Berlin: 844–47.

———. (1916). "Die Grundlage der allgemeinen Relativitätstheorie." Annalen der Physik 49 (7): 769–822.

Eisold, Kenneth. (2002). "Jung, Jungians, and Psychoanalysis." *Psychoanalytic Psychology* 19 (3): 501–24.

Emsley, John. (2000). *The 13th Element: The Sordid Tale of Murder, Fire, and Phosphorus.* New York: John Wiley and Sons.

Fogassi, Leonardo, and Vittorio Gallese. (2002). "The Neural Correlates of Action Understanding in Non-Human Primates." In *Mirror Neurons and the Evolution of Brain and Language,* edited by Maxim I. Stamenov and Vittorio Gallese, 13–35. Amsterdam, Philadelphia: John Benjamins Publishing.

Freud, Sigmund. (1933). *New Introductory Lectures on Psycho-Analysis. The Standard Edition of the Complete Psychological Works of Sigmund Freud, Volume XXII.* New York: W. W. Norton.

Frisch, Karl von. (1953). *The Dancing Bees.* Translated by Dora Ilse. New York: Harvest Book; Harcourt, Brace.

Gallese, Vittorio, Luciano Fadiga, Leonardo Fogassi, and Giacomo Rizzolatti. (1996). "Action Recognition in the Premotor Cortex." *Brain* 119: 593–609.

Gieser, Suzanne. (2005). *The Innermost Kernel.* Berlin, Heidelberg, New York: Springer.

Gleick, James. (1988). *Chaos: Making a New Science.* New York: Penguin Books.

Goldman, Alvin I. (2005). "Imitation, Mind Reading, and Simulation." In *Perspectives on Imitation: From Neuroscience to Social Science,* Vol. 2,

*Imitation, Human Development, and Culture,* edited by Susan Hurley
and Nick Chater, 79–93. Cambridge, Mass.: MIT Press.

———. (2006). *Simulating Minds: The Philosophy, Psychology, and
Neuroscience of Mindreading.* Oxford: Oxford University Press.

Greatrix, Toni S. (2002). "Projective Identification: How Does It Work?"
*Neuro-Psychoanalysis* 4 (2): 187–97.

Grotowski, Jerzy. (1968/2002). *Towards a Poor Theatre.* New York:
Routledge.

Hannah, Barbara. (1976). *Jung: His Life and Work.* New York: Perigree
Books.

Hatfield, Elaine, John T. Cacioppo, and Richard L. Rapson. (1994).
*Emotional Contagion.* Cambridge: Cambridge University Press.

Hogenson, George B. (2001). "The Baldwin Effect: A Neglected Influence on
C. G. Jung's Evolutionary Thinking." *Journal of Analytical Psychology* 46
(4): 591–611.

———. (2005). "The Self, the Symbolic, and Synchronicity: Virtual Realities
and the Emergence of the Psyche." *Journal of Analytical Psychology* 50
(3): 271–84.

Hopcke, Robert H. (1997). *There Are No Accidents: Synchronicity and the
Stories of Our Lives.* New York: Riverhead Books.

Hoyle, Fred. (1950). *The Nature of the Universe.* London: Blackwell.

———. (1957). *The Black Cloud.* New York: Harper and Brothers.

Huesmann, L. Rowell. (2005). "Imitation and the Effects of Observing
Media Violence on Behavior." In *Perspectives on Imitation: From
Neuroscience to Social Science,* Vol. 2, *Imitation, Human Development,
and Culture,* edited by Susan Hurley and Nick Chater, 257–66.
Cambridge, MA: MIT Press.

Iacoboni, Marco. (2008). *Mirroring People.* New York: Farrar, Straus and
Giroux.

Jacobi, Jolande. (1973). *The Psychology of C. G. Jung.* New Haven, Conn.: Yale
University Press.

Jacoby, Mario. (1984). *The Analytic Encounter: Transference and Human
Relationship.* Toronto: Inner City Books.

James, William. (1961). *The Varieties of Religious Experience.* New York:
Collier Books.

Jones, Ernest. (1953). *The Life and Work of Sigmund Freud,* Vol. 1, *The*

*Formative Years and the Great Discoveries, 1856–1900*. New York: Basic Books.

Jung, C. G. (1915). "On Psychological Understanding." In *The Psychogenesis of Mental Disease, Collected Works 3*. Princeton, N.J.: Princeton University Press.

———. (1929). "Problems of Modern Psychotherapy." In *The Practice of Psychotherapy, Collected Works 16*. Princeton, N.J.: Princeton University Press.

———. (1930). "Richard Wilhelm: In Memoriam." In *The Spirit in Man, Art, and Literature, Collected Works 15*. Princeton, N.J.: Princeton University Press.

———. (1934/1950). "A Study in the Process of Individuation." In *The Archetypes and the Collective Unconscious, Collected Works 9i*. Princeton, N.J.: Princeton University Press.

———. (1940). "The Psychology of the Child Archetype." In *The Archetypes and the Collective Unconscious, Collected Works 9i*. Princeton, N.J.: Princeton University Press.

———. (1945/1948). "On the Nature of Dreams." In *The Structure and Dynamics of the Psyche, Collected Works 8*. Princeton, N.J.: Princeton University Press.

———. (1946). "The Psychology of the Transference." In *The Practice of Psychotherapy, Collected Works 16*. Princeton, N.J.: Princeton University Press.

———. (1947/1954/1969). "On the Nature of the Psyche." In *The Structure and Dynamics of the Psyche, Collected Works 8*. Princeton, N.J.: Princeton University Press.

———. (1950). "Foreword to the 'I Ching.'" In *Psychology and Religion: West and East, Collected Works 11*. Princeton, N.J.: Princeton University Press.

———. (1951/1959). *Aion: Researches into the Phenomenology of the Self, Collected Works 9ii*. Princeton, N.J.: Princeton University Press.

———. (1953/1966). *Two Essays on Analytical Psychology, Collected Works 7*. Princeton, N.J.: Princeton University Press.

———. (1953/1968). *Psychology and Alchemy, Collected Works 12*. Princeton, N.J.: Princeton University Press.

———. (1956). *Symbols of Transformation, Collected Works 5*. Princeton, N.J.: Princeton University Press.

———. (1958). "Flying Saucers: A Modern Myth of Things Seen in the Skies." In *Civilization in Transition*, 2nd ed., *Collected Works 10*. Princeton, N.J.: Princeton University Press.

———. (1960). "Synchronicity: An Acausal Connecting Principle." In *The Structure and Dynamics of the Psyche, Collected Works 8*. Princeton, N.J.: Princeton University Press.

———. (1963). *Memories, Dreams, Reflections*. New York: Pantheon.

———. (1970). *Civilization in Transition*, 2nd ed., *Collected Works 10*. Princeton, N.J.: Princeton University Press.

———. (1971). *Psychological Types, Collected Works 6*. Princeton, N.J.: Princeton University Press.

———. (1975). *Letters*, Vol. 2, *1951–1961*, Edited by Gerhard Adler and Aniela Jaffé. Princeton, N.J.: Princeton University Press.

Jung, C. G. (1984). *Dream Analysis*. Edited by William McGuire. Princeton: Princeton University Press.

Jung, C. G., and Wolfgang Pauli. (1955). *The Interpretation of Nature and the Psyche*. New York: Pantheon Books.

Keil, Frank, C. and Robert Andrew Wilson, eds. (2001). *The MIT Encyclopedia of the Cognitive Sciences*. Cambridge, Mass.: MIT Press.

Kim, Jaegwon. (1993). *Supervenience and Mind*. Cambridge: Cambridge University Press.

Knox, Jean. (2003). *Archetype, Attachment, Analysis*. Hove and New York: Brunner-Routledge.

Koestler, Arthur. (1971). *The Case of the Midwife Toad*. New York: Random House.

Kohut, Heinz. (1984). *How Does Analysis Cure?* Chicago: University of Chicago Press.

Lammers, Ann Conrad. (2007). "Jung and White and the God of Terrible Double Aspect." *Journal of Analytical Psychology* 52 (3): 253–74.

Lammers, Ann Conrad, and Adrian Cunningham, eds. (2007). *The Jung-White Letters*. London and New York: Routledge.

Lipps, T. (1900). "Aesthetische Einfühlung." *Zeitschrift für Psychologie und Physiologie der Sinnesorgane* 22: 415–50.

———. (1903). "Einfhlung, innere Nachahmung, und Organempfin-dungen." *Archiv für die gesamte Psychologie* 1: 185–204.

————. (1905). "Weiteres zur Einfühlung." *Archiv für die gesamte Psychologie* 4: 465–519.

————. (1907). "Psychologie und Asthetik." *Archiv für die gesamte Psychologie* 9: 91–116.

————. (1908). "Aesthetik." In *Die Kultur der Gegenwart: Ihre Entwicklung und ihr Ziele,* edited by P. Hinneberg. Berlin: Teubner.

————. (1913). "Zur Einfühlung." In *Psychologische Studien,* Band. 2, edited by T. Lipps. Leipzig: Engelmann.

Lotze, Rudolf Hermann. (1874). *Logik.* System der Philosophie, I. Leipzig.

Main, Roderick, selection and introduction. (1997). *Encountering Jung: On Synchronicity and the Paranormal.* Princeton, N.J.: Princeton University Press.

————. (2004). *The Rupture of Time: Synchronicity and Jung's Critique of Modern Western Culture.* Hove and New York: Brunner-Routledge.

————. (2007). *Revelations of Chance: Synchronicity as Spiritual Experience.* Albany: State University of New York Press.

Mainzer, Klaus. (2005). *Symmetry and Complexity.* Hackensack, N.J.: World Scientific.

Mansfield, Victor. (1995). *Synchronicity, Science, and Soul-Making.* Chicago and La Salle: Open Court Press.

Manville, Brook, and Josiah Ober. (2003). *A Company of Citizens,* 55–86. Boston: Harvard Business School Press.

Marias, Eugene. (1971). *The Soul of the White Ant.* Translated by Winifred de Kok. London: Jonathan Cape, and Anthony Blond.

Martindale, Diane. (2000). "Beetle to Bee." *Scientific American* 283 (1): 26.

Martin-Vallas, François. (2006). "The Transferential Chimera: A Clinical Approach." *Journal of Analytical Psychology* 51 (5): 627–41.

————. (2008). "The Transferential Chimera: Some Theoretical Considerations." *Journal of Analytical Psychology* 53 (1): 37–59.

Mayer, Elizabeth L. (2002). "Freud and Jung: The Boundaried Mind and the Radically Connected Mind." *Journal of Analytical Psychology* 47 (1): 91–99.

————. (2007). *Extraordinary Knowing.* New York: Bantam Dell.

McDowell, Maxim. (2001). "Principle of Organization: A Dynamic-Systems View of the Archetype-as-Such." *Journal of Analytical Psychology* 46 (4): 637–54.

McGuire, William, ed. (1974). *The Freud/Jung Letters.* Princeton, N.J.: Princeton University Press.

Meier, Carl Alfred, ed., with the assistance of C. P. Enz and M. Fierz; translated from the German by David Roscoe; with an introductory essay by Beverley Zabriskie. (2001). *Atom and Archetype: The Pauli/Jung Letters, 1932–1958.* Princeton, N.J.: Princeton University Press.

Meier, Christian. (1990). *The Greek Discovery of Politics.* Cambridge, Mass.: Harvard University Press.

Merton, Robert K., and Elinor Barber. (2004). *The Travels and Adventures of Serendipity: A Study in Sociological Semantics and the Sociology of Science.* Princeton, N.J.: Princeton University Press.

Meyers, Morton A. (2007). *Happy Accidents: Serendipity in Modern Medical Breakthroughs.* New York: Arcade Publishing.

Morell, Virginia. (2008). "Inside Animal Minds." *National Geographic,* March issue.

Morowitz, Harold J. (2002). *The Emergence of Everything.* New York: Oxford University Press.

Mumford, David, Caroline Series, and David Wright. (2002). *Indra's Pearls: The Vision of Felix Klein.* Cambridge: Cambridge University Press.

Needham, Joseph. (1956). *Science and Civilisation in China,* Vol. 2, *History of Scientific Thought.* Cambridge: Cambridge University Press.

Neumann, Erich. (1954). *Origins and History of Consciousness.* Princeton, N.J.: Princeton University Press.

Nichol, Lee, ed. (2003). *The Essential David Bohm.* London and New York: Routledge.

Nicholson, Henry B. (2001). *Topiltzin Quetzalcoatl: The Once and Future Lord of the Toltecs.* Boulder: University Press of Colorado.

Obeyesekere, Gananath. (1992). *The Apotheosis of Captain Cook: European Mythmaking in the Pacific.* Princeton, N.J.: Princeton University Press.

Onians, Richard Broxton. (1951/1988). *The Origins of European Thought about the Body, the Mind, the Soul, the World, Time, and Fate,* Cambridge: Cambridge University Press.

Pauli, Wolfgang. (1955). "The Influence of Archetypal Ideas on the Scientific Theories of Kepler." In *The Interpretation of Nature and the Psyche,* by C. G. Jung and W. Pauli. New York: Pantheon Books.

Peat, F. David. (1987). *Synchronicity: The Bridge between Matter and Mind.* New York: Bantam Books.

Pigman, George, W. (1995). "Freud and the History of Empathy." *International Journal of Psycho-Analysis* 76: 237–56.

Prinz, Jesse. (2005). "Imitation and Moral Development." In *Perspectives on Imitation: From Neuroscience to Social Science,* Vol. 2, *Imitation, Human Development, and Culture,* edited by Susan Hurley and Nick Chater, 267–82. Cambridge: MIT Press.

Ramachandran, Vilayanur S. (2004). *A Brief Tour of Human Consciousness.* New York: Pi Press.

Remer, Theodore G., ed. (1965). *Serendipity and the Three Princes: From the Peregrinaggio of 1557.* Norman: University of Oklahoma Press.

Richardson, Robert. (2006). *William James: In the Maelstrom of American Modernism.* Boston: Houghton Mifflin.

Rizzolatti, Giacomo, Laila Craighero, and Luciano Fadiga. (2002). "The Mirror System in Humans." In *Mirror Neurons and the Evolution of Brain and Language,* edited by Maxim I. Stamenov and Vittorio Gallese, 37–59. Amsterdam, Philadelphia: John Benjamins Publishing.

Sahlins, Marshall. (1995). *How "Natives" Think: About Captain Cook, for Example.* Chicago: University of Chicago Press.

Samuels, Andrew. (1985). *Jung and the Post-Jungians.* London, Boston, Melbourne and Henley: Routledge and Kegan Paul.

Samuels, A., B. Shorter, and F. Plaut. (1986) *A Critical Dictionary of Jungian Analysis.* London: Routledge.

Sandler, Joseph. (1998). "Countertransference and Role-Responsiveness." In *Enactment: Toward a New Approach to the Therapeutic Relationship,* edited by Steven J. Ellman and Michael Moskowitz, 29–36. Northvale, N.J.: Jason Aronson.

Saunders, Peter, and Patricia Skar. (2001). "Archetypes, Complexes, and Self-Organization." *Journal of Analytical Psychology* 46 (2): 305–23.

Sawyer, R. Keith. (2005). *Social Emergence: Societies as Complex Systems.* Cambridge: Cambridge University Press.

Schattschneider, Doris. (2004). *M. C. Escher: Visions of Symmetry.* New York: Harry N. Abrams.

Schwartz-Salant, Nathan. (1989). *The Borderline Personality: Vision and Healing.* Wilmette, Ill.: Chiron Publications.

Singer, Tania, Ben Seymour, John O'Doherty, Holger Kaube, Raymond J. Dolan, and Chris D. Frith. (2004). "Empathy for Pain Involves the Affective but Not Sensory Components of Pain." *Science* 303 (5661): 1157–62.

Singer, Tania, and Chris Frith. (2005). "The Painful Side of Empathy." *Nature Neuroscience* 8 (7): 845–46.

Singh, Simon. (2004). *Big Bang: The Origins of the Universe.* New York: HarperCollins.

Solomon, Hester. (2007). *The Self in Transformation.* London: Karnac.

Spitz, René, (1959). *A Genetic Field Theory of Ego Formation.* New York: International University Press.

Surowiecki, James. (2004). *The Wisdom of Crowds.* New York: Doubleday.

Sutton, Lilian. (2008). "Addiction: Between Paradise and Hell, the Challenge of Maintaining the Tensions." Presented at the *Journal of Analytical Psychology*'s VIIIth International Conference, Tradition and Creativity: Reframing Analysis in a Changing World. Lake Orta, Italy, 17 May 2008.

Tresan, David. (1996). "Jungian Metapsychology and Neurobiological Theory." *Journal of Analytical Psychology* 41 (3): 399–436.

Van Baaren, R. B., R. W. Holland, K. Kawakami, and A. van Knippenberg. (2004). "Mimicry and Pro-Social Behavior." *Psychological Science* 15: 71–74.

Vischer, Robert. (1873). *Über das optische Formgefuhl: Ein Beitrag zur Aesthetik* (*On the Optical Sense of Form: A Contribution to Aesthetics*). Leipzig: Credner.

von Franz, Marie-Louise. (1974). *Number and Time: Reflections Leading toward a Unification of Depth Psychology and Physics.* Translated by Andrea Dykes. Evanston, Ill.: Northwestern University Press.

———. (1980). *On Divination and Synchronicity: The Psychology of Meaningful Chance.* Toronto: Inner City Books.

———. (1992). *Psyche and Matter.* Boston and London: Shambhala.

Waltham, Clae. (1971). *Chuang Tzu: Genius of the Absurd,* arranged from the work of James Legge. New York: Ace Books.

Wiktionary. (2008). "Daimon." Retrieved 19 July 2008 from http://en.wiktionary.org/wiki/.

Wilford, John Nobel. (2007). "In Medieval Architecture, Signs of Advanced Math." *New York Times,* 27 February.

Wilhelm, Helmut. (1943). "Leibniz and the *I-Ching*." *Collectanea Commissionis Synodalis in Sinis* 16: 205–19.

Wilkinson, Margaret. (2006). *Coming into Mind*. New York: Routledge.

Williams, L. Pearce. (1980). *The Origins of Field Theory*. Lanham, Md.: University Press of America.

Wimmer, Heinz, and Josef Perner. (1983). "Beliefs about Beliefs: Representation and Constraining Function of Wrong Beliefs in Young Children's Understanding of Deception." *Cognition* 12: 103–28.

Yates, Frances A. (1966). *The Art of Memory*. Chicago: University of Chicago Press.

# Index